PRACTICAL, PROVEN, POWERFUL STRATEGIES
TO BUILD RESILIENCY AND MANAGE YOUR MOST
CHALLENGING LIFE AND WORK STRUGGLES

THE FINKELSTEIN FACTOR™

WHAT TO DO WHEN THINGS GO WRONG...
BECAUSE YOU KNOW THEY WILL (SIGH)

MARION GROBB FINKELSTEIN

Though based on true stories, details of many of the case studies shared have been changed or combined to create composite characters and preserve the privacy of individuals. Others are completely fictitious and presented as examples only.

Text Copyright © 2019 by Marion Grobb Finkelstein

All rights reserved. No part of this book may be reproduced in any form or by any means, or stored in a database or retrieval system, without prior express written permission from the publisher except for brief quotations embodied in critical essay, article, or review. These articles and/or reviews must state the correct title and author of this book by name. If you would like permission to use this book other than for review purposes, please contact marion@marionspeaks.com Thank you in advance for your support of the author's rights.

Published by MarionSpeaks™
Niagara Falls, Ontario, Canada
www.MarionSpeaks.com
Marion@MarionSpeaks.com

MarionSpeaks™ provides a variety of conference keynotes and on-site workshops for clients. To find out more, contact MarionSpeaks™ or go to www.MarionSpeaks.com

ISBNs: 978-1-7752484-5-3 (Canadian audio); 978-1-7752484-3-9 (Canadian paperback book); 978-1-7752484-4-6 (Canadian ebook)

Subjects: Success in business, motivation (psychology), motivational

Jacket design by Debbie Bishop
Jacket © 2019 copyright by MarionSpeaks™

Book design by Debbie Bishop

Printed in the United States of America

Bulk book orders are available at special quantity discounts to use as premiums and sales promotions or for use in corporate training programs. To order or enquire contact marion@marionspeaks.com or visit www.marionspeaks.com

Disclaimer: This book is a compilation of ideas from the author. As such, they are suggestions only and to be used at the sole discretion of the reader. No results are guaranteed and examples used are anecdotal and for illustrative purposes only.

CONTENTS

LETTER TO THE READER	v
CHAPTER 1: Finkelstein Factor™ explained	1
CHAPTER 2: Why self-care is selfless	5
Victim vs. victor mindset	6
If you need additional help, get it	9
SELF CARE PRINCIPLE: don't give until it hurts; just give until it feels good	12
SELF CARE PRINCIPLE: The power of choice	16
SELF-CARE PRINCIPLE: If you don't take care of yourself, someone else might	24
SELF-CARE PRINCIPLE: You can't give what you don't have	29
SELF-CARE PRINCIPLE: You're worth it	30
SELF-CARE PRINCIPLE: Love isn't limited	38
SELF-CARE ACID TEST: Three tests to measure your degree of self-care and decide if it's time for more	40
Chapter 2 recap	43
CHAPTER 3	45
STEP 1: ACKNOWLEDGE YOUR LOSS — What's your problem?	
LOSS PRINCIPLE: your situation robs you of your goals	46
LOSS PRINCIPLE: life isn't controllable (your responses are)	50
LOSS PRINCIPLE: admitting hurt is a strength	52
LOSS PRINCIPLE: acknowledging losses validates your pain	52
YOUR TURN: what is your loss?	56
LOSS PRINCIPLE: understand others by acknowledging their loss	59
How to word it	60
Chapter 3 recap	62

CONTENTS

CHAPTER 4 — 63
STEP 2, Q1:
WHAT'S MY ROLE?
Replay please (without guilt or regret)

- What's your real-life example? — 64
- How you contribute to your negative outcome — 66
- An explanation isn't an excuse — 75
- Keep the memory, leave the emotion — 75
- Acknowledge and then forgive — 77
- Chapter 4 recap — 78

CHAPTER 5 — 79
STEP 2, Q2:
HOW COULD IT BE WORSE?
Develop an attitude of gratitude

- Debbie's divorce — 82
- Flirtatious Frank — 83
- Steve's bus bust — 84
- So what's the "DIF"? — 87
- Marion's disc disaster — 89
- How to word it — 93
- Chapter 5 recap — 96

CHAPTER 6 — 99
STEP 2, Q3:
WHAT'S THE GIFT?
Reaping the reward

- What exactly is "a gift"? — 100
- How to unwrap your gift — 101
- There are many types of gifts — 110
- How to word it — 111
- Chapter 6 recap — 113

CHAPTER 7 — 115

STEP 2, Q4:
WHAT WILL YOU CHANGE IN FUTURE?
Move knowledge to action

Your lessons are transferable	116
Apply your lessons in future	118
You are the creator of your own reality	121
How to word it	122
Chapter 7 recap	123

CHAPTER 8 — 125

STEP 3:
LET GO
Release the pain

Principle of letting go: Hanging on to the past keeps you tethered to the ground	125
Principle of letting go: It takes as much energy to hang on to the past as to move forward into the future	127
How to let go	129
Chapter 8 recap	140

CHAPTER 9: Final thoughts — 141

What resonates with you, you were meant to hear	141
One small change, one big difference	142
Move knowledge to action	143
Read again, learn again	144
Feedback welcome	144
Before we leave	145

About the author — 147

LETTER TO THE READER
A message from Marion

Welcome, I'm glad you're here!

You are reading this book for a reason. Possibly you are seeking answers to your questions about how to handle tough situations and people. Maybe you are currently going through a difficult time and need some support and a change of perspective to cope. Or perhaps you know someone who is grappling to stay afloat and you are looking for a lifesaver to throw them in the form of tools and techniques you could share. All these things are available for taking in these pages.

As a former Director Communications at national museums, international airports, and Canadian federal government organizations, I have lots of experience in communicating with individuals and the masses. This background, along with my academic education and certifications in personality type, have provided me with tremendous insights into human behaviour. All this is wonderful and prepared me to develop the systems I'll be sharing with you to help you build your resiliency and handle life's difficult moments.

That being said, it's important to note that my expertise is that of communication. I am not a medical professional of any sort and my suggestions made between these covers are not intended to replace medical treatment of any sort. As useful as the processes

LETTER TO THE READER

I share may be, they aren't a panacea for everything that ails you. Depending on the nature and severity of your circumstances, you may wish to seek additional support. While this book and the principles I share may give you a process and many techniques to lessen the pain, certain conditions clearly go beyond the scope of this book, I leave it to you to seek out and get whatever degree of professional support you need.

Likewise, adopting the techniques and strategies I suggest are strictly at your own discretion. Although I have found them to be useful and proven in most cases, there are no guarantees how much they will serve you.

Keep an open mind, surrender to the process, and give the exercises a go. I am confident they will help because my clients tell me they do and because they help *me* every day. Yes, I actually use them. They will help you too.

Real-life stories will help you understand how these systems you will be learning actually apply and how they work. You may find yourself relating to the examples shared--I hope you do. I hope they resonate with you and touch your very core. These stories and real and raw and share intimate details of people's lives. In the interest of confidentiality, names and circumstances have been changed to maintain the privacy of the individuals involved. The lessons remain.

Reaching out for help is one of the principles I mention throughout this book. In that spirit, I reached out to a handful of valued colleagues to request their comments and input on my draft writings. This book is better because of their input, eagle eyes, insight, and constructive suggestions. In alphabetical order, great, big editing thanks go out to Holly Bridges, Lianna Carlisle, Corina Deguire, Emily Flesher, Laurie Flasko, Chris Ford, Shelley Hoye,

Sutcliffe. And as long as I'm doling out thank yous, a bow of appreciation to my hubby, Steve Finkelstein, who was the inspiration for *The Finkelstein Factor*™ and so much happiness in my life.

I certainly don't profess to have all the answers. What I share has worked for me and others and I hope it will also push you forward.

Take my hand as I guide you through a process to change your mindset and your results. Here's to a productive journey as you explore *The Finkelstein Factor*™ and discover what to do when things go wrong ... because you know they will (sigh).

CHAPTER 1

FINKELSTEIN FACTOR™ EXPLAINED

What the heck is "Finkelstein Factor™"?

Picture yourself on a trip where everything goes wrong. Your baggage gets lost. Your flight is delayed. You're traveling with another couple and they get the huge suite room while you get the room by the daily laundry cart run. Your in-room security deposit box lock is broken. You step on a rusty nail in the bathroom. Your excursion includes a choice of cocktails but they only have one available. Your return flight charges you for extra luggage weight. Something hits your intestines on the return flight home and you spend the entire trip running to and from the airplane bathroom. Get the gist?

Every single one of those things has happened to my husband, Steve Finkelstein, several times. So much so that a few years ago, when something went wonky, I started attributing it to what I call, *The Finkelstein Factor™*. Hence, the term was coined.

"The FInkelstein Factor™ is at play when nothing seems to go your way".
~Marion Grobb Finkelstein

You might not know it by this name but you surely know the syndrome. *The Finkelstein Factor™* is at play those days when nothing seems to go your way. You keep on plodding ahead, do all the right things, and yet it seems the world conspires against you to mess it all up. When something unexpected happens that throws you off balance and for a loop, that right there, is the *Finkelstein Factor*™.

Watching Steve move through large and small life challenges with grace and humour prompted me to question how I was handling my own trying times. It gave me pause to reflect on how he managed to flip negative circumstances into positive outcomes with seeming ease while I was spiraling downward. That's not to say it was easy for him--it's to note that he handled similar circumstances differently than many people, including me. That was an ah-ha moment for me--the key was in *how he responded*.

Being a systems-oriented person, I began to break down Steve's actions and attitude into bite-size steps and processes. This afforded me the opportunity to notice my own thought patterns and behaviours. I became more aware and mindful of what I was thinking, saying, and doing, and the impact that these actions had on my outcomes, including how I felt. The result was resetting my perspective, recalibrating my mindset, and transforming how I handled challenges. Changing how I was thinking and what I was doing was creating more of the results I wanted to see. Soon my clients were also using the systems I share with you here and they too saw results.

In working with others and applying the principles and strategies to my own life, I soon learned that the *Finkelstein Factor*™ isn't just about unfortunate incidents occurring: It is about finding ways to handle them. Over a number of years, I introduced various exercises and systems into my training sessions that eventually became parts of the processes featured in this book. Each question and step you will find has been designed to help you flip your mindset to more positive and to boost your coping skills and resiliency.

The principles you will learn in the following pages will help you in both your professional and personal lives. By shifting mindsets and perspectives, they have helped hundreds of my clients manage budget cuts, bad appraisals, tough clients, and bully bosses. You'll read about many of these case studies in the following pages. Whether in your work or private life, you have the ability to handle your challenges--you just need to be shown how and that's what I plan to do.

You may attribute not only slight irritants you face in life to the *Finkelstein Factor*™: It also applies to life-altering events such as job losses, troublesome employees, broken marriages, accidents, illnesses, and the loss of loved ones. Perhaps these adversities are wreaking havoc in your own life right now. Regardless of the scope or nature of your challenge, understanding *The Finkelstein Factor*™ and gaining the skills to handle life's adversities, will help you bounce, not back, but forward.

Like you, I am no stranger to difficult situations and have faced many struggles in my life. I know what it means to feel stuck, negative, and angry. I've tasted that frustration of wanting to change my outcomes in both my personal and professional lives and not knowing how. That's why I decided to write a book with hands-on tips, proven strategies, and a systematic process to guide you through a challenge and boost your coping skills. I want to help you jump over the years of trial and error I lived and skip right to the part about solutions.

People often ask me how I came up with *The Finkelstein Factor*™ and all the approaches I'm giving you now. The real truth is that they are borne of my own hardships and desperation to find relief.

The study of neuroplasticity, researchers, and scientists tell us that we have the ability to relearn and train our brains to follow new and different pathways. This is exciting news because it means you're not stuck in your thinking if you don't want to be. If your mindset is holding you back, you can learn a different way to act and think that will better serve you.

I developed these *Flip It Formula*™ trademarked steps as part of the *Finkelstein Factor*™ to help cope, move forward, and out of my own necessity to manage my own challenges and disappointments in life. Now, they help others, including you. My survival instinct guided my head in thinking of them, my heart in feeling them, and my hand in putting them into action and committing them to written form so you might benefit.

I have handpicked my most popular and effective systems to help you in your journey. These are the approaches I've honed in dozens of workshops with hundreds of clients. With their feedback and using the techniques myself, I've refined the process into digestible chunks you can wrap your head around. In the following chapters, you'll find out more about what inspired this book and how these systems have helped as you hear Steve's, my, and other people's real-life stories.

In the next chapter, we're going to really dig deep and create the foundation for you to solidly build your way forward. How you communicate with others begins with how you talk to yourself, and your self-talk reveals a great deal about how you value *you*. Let's see how much you care for yourself … or not.

CHAPTER 2

WHY SELF-CARE IS SELFLESS

Get ready for the Finkelstein Factor™ fix

Like many people, you may have been raised to believe that putting yourself first is distasteful, even selfish. Perhaps you were told that giving to others to the point of making yourself ill, or compromising your own health, well-being, happiness, or financial future is somehow honourable. There are some people who actually consider putting themselves at constant risk as charity. Are you one of these people? Do you push your own needs to the background even when no one is expecting or asking you to do so?

> "You can't fill someone else's glass if yours is empty".
> ~Marion Grobb Finkelstein

I invite you to challenge that thinking. Taking care of yourself isn't selfish at all. In fact, it *ensures* that you have the energy, health, time, and sustainable resources to care for others. Take the example of seeing someone drowning: If you jump in and aren't strong enough to rescue him or her, you both drown. Get yourself safe, secure, and on solid ground and then reach out to save. Taking care of yourself puts you in a position to safely and effectively care for others.

By the end of this book, there's a good chance you will have the skills and shift in perspective to see your situation differently, to understand that your needless suffering doesn't help anyone, including yourself. It's time to take care of yourself first because you matter and others need you in their lives.

Shifting your thinking from victim to victor begins with your mindset.

Victim vs. victor mindset

Let me make a distinction: Being a "victim" and having a "victim mindset" are two different things.

You can't be a victim unless you allow yourself to become one and truly believe that you are one. You may be targeted unfairly. You may be used and abused. You may be given nasty rolls of the dice in your life. These are all horrible events and none of them define you unless you allow them to do that. *You* define who you are. The event doesn't have the power to determine who you are. Your unfortunate situation, whatever it is that you're struggling with, is something that is happening in your life--it's not you.

How you *respond* to injustices in life is what defines you. If you feel like a victim, or have ever felt that way in the past, know that you can change your mindset from victim to victor simply by changing your thinking. You have a victor inside: You just have to shout it out and get it out!

What holds you in the victim role (PS: it's not worth it)

In contrast to the mindset of a victor, a victim feels powerless, hopeless, and is only ever in reaction mode. Do you routinely feel this way? The skill to change this feeling comes in developing the tools and techniques you need to ensure that these moments don't become days, weeks, and years. Following are a few reasons why some people hang on to the victim mindset and find it incredibly difficult to see themselves in the light of a victor. You may relate.

Attention from others

If you're stuck in the victim mindset and lean toward extroversion, you may regale others with your tales of your woe. You find yourself sharing sad details of your struggles with others and receiving expressions of support and sympathy.

In contrast, if you have a preference for introversion, when friends ask how it's going, you may stoically answer, "fine", even though they, and you, know it's not. You commend yourself for keeping a stiff upper lip and find it rewarding that surely they see you as strong and a non-complainer.

In the short-term, the payoff of getting this attention feels good but in the long-term, it feeds the cycle of you placing yourself in the victim role. You are perpetuating the behaviour that is actually hurting you. Attention from others, even if it's born more from pity than admiration, is a shallow reward that holds some people mired in the victim mindset.

It's known and familiar to you

Even though you may not want to be known as a victim, and although you might cognitively recognize that it's not a healthy place to be, you easily slip into a pattern of enabling this dance because it may be the only one you know. This pattern is sadly familiar to you and you repeat it often because you find familiar comfort in your discomfort. Whether you realize it or not, this isn't what you deserve: You have earned much more. Just because a role you've played up until now is familiar, doesn't mean it's the right one for you.

You surround yourself with victim mentality

If allowed, your victim sentiment becomes contagious. You carry negative energy forward and spread it wherever you find a listening ear. You surround yourself with other willing enablers who support and feed into what some may call your pity party. You are surrounding yourself with other people who also assume a victim mentality and you find a solace in not being alone in your misery. TIP: get a new circle of support--a positive one!

Victors choose their mindset and role

Perhaps you are swamped at work and find it relieves your stress to catch up on files in your own time. You might consider yourself a victim, *oh poor me*. However, a more empowering mindset and that of a victor recognizes you are *choosing* your mindset, actions, and reactions. You *choose* to give up your precious quiet evenings--that doesn't make you a victim. That makes you a decision-maker of what your role will be. Own your decision and be proud of it. That feeling of empowerment you get takes you out of the victim mindset and instantly shifts you to that of a victor.

While someone with a victim mindset may find it less painful to put more work and stress on her own shoulders rather than disappoint or anger someone else, a victor balances the needs of others with their own equally important needs. Sure, she might choose to take those extra files one weekend, but it won't be at the expense of everything and everyone else important in her life. A victor mindfully

> "The one thing you always control is your mindset".
> ~Marion Grobb Finkelstein

exercises the power of choice with balance as a guiding principle. A victor actively chooses her mindset and role rather than having them imposed upon her.

If you need additional help, get it

Before we go further, I'm compelled to address severe situations that go beyond the purview of this book. Although I know the systems and processes I'm going to share in the coming chapters work in many situations, these approaches are not the panacea for every condition. You may find yourself in a situation that is so severe you want to supplement the approaches discussed in this book with additional professional medical treatment. There is great strength and wisdom in seeking what you need. Kudos to you for seeking assistance and solutions instead of staying stuck.

> "Asking for help is a strength, not a weakness ...
> You deserve the support."
> ~Marion Grobb Finkelstein

The point is this: Seek the help you deserve and don't stop until you find the right solution for you. Whether that be this book alone or my suggestions supplemented with the expertise and guidance of healthcare professionals.

As you read this chapter, you'll understand why self-care of any sort is healthy and makes tremendous sense for you and everyone in your life. For now, let's explore a couple of situations where you may wish to get supplemental support beyond this book. These examples certainly aren't all-inclusive and are offered simply as examples of situations that are more common than you may realize. Everyone has challenges, the difference is in the severity and how we handle them.

Ever feel like giving up? (Learned helplessness)

The field of psychology has coined the term, "learned helplessness". This is when you put energy and action into removing yourself from toxic situations or bad decisions, and every time you do, you feel beaten to the ground. You learn, after many efforts, that your attempts seem to be in vain and result in no change. Eventually, you give up and reach a point where you don't even try anymore. You figure, *why bother?* You surrender your happiness to circumstances you see as beyond your control. The sad thing is that the circumstance or person holding you back may no longer be an obstacle or respond in the way you've learned and come to expect they would, and hence, they no longer hold that power over you. Sadly, you will never know that because you've given up trying.

Think of the extreme case of an abused person or the battered spouse syndrome. The beatings may be physical or psychological, either being deplorable. After weeks, months and years of this treatment, you learn that any response you receive will be negative, followed by seemingly sincere apologies until another trigger is pulled and the cycle begins again. Instead of leaving, you modify your behaviour to avoid that action you believe will spark the abusive response. Rather than recognizing it's the other person's behaviour that is the problem, you begin to think it's you. It makes no logical sense at all, yet it's the way you've learned to behave and it's all you can see through your clouded lens.

At this moment, you don't realize you have options because the abuse has happened for so long and warped your perception. Your world has shrunk and your thinking is contained within a very limited box. You have been targeted and no longer give yourself permission to spread your wings and fly high. Everything you do and say is carefully designed to avoid the unwarranted punishment you've come to expect. You are coming from a place of fear and rather than spending your energy to seek pleasure, you channel it to avoid pain. You have a misguided sense of commitment to stay in the relationship telling yourself it's love holding you together. (It's not).

If you relate to these conditions, you may well have *learned helplessness* and may benefit from resources beyond what I have to offer. I encourage you to get them.

Depression is debilitating

Apart from learned helplessness, another very serious and common challenge you may face at various points in your life is that feeling of overwhelming depression. I'm not talking about blue moments or a funk that lasts a day or two. Rather, you find yourself unable to lift yourself from the quicksand that keeps you pulled into the depths of despair. Activities you once found enjoyable now bring no pleasure at all. You have little interest in daily routines such as getting dressed, making meals, or going to work. It takes a herculean effort to get out of bed. Whether you are experiencing postpartum depression or struggling with chronic or episodic stressful events in your life, all these things have the immense ability to pull you into a profound depression and loss of hope.

Chances are your situation isn't as dire as it appears. Even beyond physical environment and conditions, the one thing you always control is your mindset. I'm going to explore that in the following chapters and show you how to rewire your thinking to chase out those cobwebs and old thinking patterns that are bringing you down. If these techniques alone aren't enough, professional medical care is always another option. It could be something as simple as short-term medication or counseling to boost you over the hump. There is no reason to suffer any longer.

Post-traumatic stress disorder
(You deserve professional help)

There is another completely different group of people who are in excruciating pain, though the severity of their injuries may lay dormant for some time. These are the brave souls who live with what psychologists call *post-traumatic stress disorder (PTSD)*. If you are one of these individuals, you suffer from huge, life-altering and damaging events so extreme in nature they leave an indelible scar. No one gets over this alone. You have been deeply injured and intense multi-faceted healthcare will help you move to a healthy place. Now it the time to get it. Get whatever support you need to feel whole and happy again. This is what self-care is all about: getting yourself taken care of so you can properly take care of others.

SELF-CARE PRINCIPLE: Don't give until it hurts; just give until it feels good.

When you take care of yourself as much as you do others, you empower yourself, build confidence, and gain skills to competently navigate through life's challenges.

The danger of being a giver

If you're falling into the trap of giving to the point of depleting all your resources, you're not helping yourself or others. In fact, you are crippling both yourself and those you think you're serving. When you exhaust your reserves, be they time, energy, finances or any other, you place yourself in a precarious and stressful situation unnecessarily. You set yourself up for a fall and perhaps even resentment for all you gave and gave up. You put pressure on those around you to be thankful even when they didn't ask for your sacrifice.

In the office, it's been my experience that it's often the women who initiate the life celebrations and parties, pass around the anniversary cards, and buy the farewell gifts. You coddle and care, protect and defend, all in the name of love and collegial support. You get so good at it, taking care of others becomes second nature to you. Sadly, this is often done with complete disregard for your own needs and desires. When was the last time you let someone else's preferences and choices override yours? My guess is you have many examples ranging from giving someone else the larger piece of cake, to putting your career on hold to accommodate your spouse climbing the ladder, your children attending college, or your elderly parents receiving the care you believe they are owed. But at what price to yourself?

Karen's message

When I was in my early thirties, I was doing the marketing and promotions for a national museum in Ottawa, Ontario. Every year, the United Way Campaign was a big event with fundraising goals and presentations. This particular year, all the employees are gathered in the auditorium and listening to Karen, one of our own colleagues, recount her experience with painful arthritis and how much United Way has helped her. It is impactful hearing a personal story from someone we all know and trust.

Although I have worked with this lady for several years, I never knew of her personal struggles. She works in sponsorship and I am in communications, so our paths cross frequently, yet I had never seen this side of her. By sharing this very human story, she makes me feel so much more connected to her. I'm confident her presentation results in people wanting to give.

I will never forget Karen's final words. In closing, she looks earnestly at the crowd and advises us, "Don't give until it hurts—just give until it feels good."

This story vividly drives home the important lesson of giving without putting yourself in jeopardy. *Don't give until it hurts--just give until it feels good.* Karen was talking about maintaining a balance between helping others and taking care of yourself. The message I took away and invite you to also get is that you can give to and help others without hurting yourself. Karen was talking about self-care.

SELF-CARE CAUTION: Your sweet intentions may turn to bitter resentment.

How many times have you seen people, perhaps yourself, give and give and give until they are depleted? Then, maybe not right away but somewhere down the road, they resent it. They gave so much that they're now suffering horribly. Or the people they gave to are ungrateful and show no sign of reciprocity. The good acts are all but forgotten and the good-deed-doers are left to wallow in their self-created misery. It's not right and it's not the way it should be. People don't always respond in the way you hope or the way you would. When you paint a perfect picture of sunshine and lollipops and real life comes up short, that gap is filled with disappointment at best and resentment at worst.

Barb and Brian's BBQs

For decades, Barb and Brian host wonderful summertime barbecues for friends, family, and neighbours. Over the years, popularity of this annual get-together grows to the point of seventy guests. The kids play in the lake, kick around soccer balls, and fling frisbees while the adults mix and mingle, sip beverages, and lounge in comfy patio chairs dotting the waterfront backyard.

Barb begins months in advance buying all the ingredients and planning the menu. Brian helps her with the tedious preparations of burgers, chicken, ribs, and a variety of salads and desserts. Although they take great delight in treating their guests, there's no denying that there is cost and labour involved. It's work.

Barb and Brian prepare as much as they can in advance and the day of the barbecue, they mix the punches and fire up the grill. Most guests arrive with a bottle of wine or hosting gift of some sort--a gesture Barb and Brian greatly appreciate as it recognizes their effort. Meanwhile, it catches their notice that others arrive empty-handed, year after year, and neither do these people ever reciprocate the hospitality in any way. No card of thanks, no invitation to their place, no token hostess gift, nothing.

Barb begins to feel the bitter taste of resentment. She notes that, in all these years of having these people in their residence for both winter and summer parties, she's never seen the inside of some of these guest's homes. They both realize that their sweet intentions haven't been appreciated by everyone.

The following year, Barb and Brian decide to forego their annual summer party. Instead, they pick and choose the friends to invite for dinner and social events throughout the year--the friends, family, and colleagues who reciprocate their efforts.

A month before their normal BBQ time, Barb and Brian are amused that several of the never-been-in-their-house guests contact them to ask when the party will be so they can be sure to mark it in their calendar. Barb and Brian feel a twinge of delight telling them that there is no party this year.

Instead of doing something they realize they resent, Barb and Brian rechannel their energies into people and activities that bring them joy.

If you see yourself in Barb and Brian's story, maybe you're also giving too much. Consider pulling back just a bit. Soon as you feel a sting of resentment, that's your signal to stop while your actions still come from a place of love and support versus anger and bitterness. No need to live in a world of bitterness and hurt.

SELF-CARE ACID TEST: If you're giving to the point of resentment or self-damage, that's your signal to pull back.

If you're a chronic giver who suffers because of it, acknowledge and change that behaviour. Still give, just a little less. Give within your means. Step back and honestly ask yourself if you're giving too much, if a little piece inside of you currently resents doing something. Or do you feel a pinch of anger about a series of events you've graced to an ungrateful recipient? If you see a pattern there, stop doing it. Recognize the dance and change up the steps. When you do, the other person can't help but change his or her steps too. If you're going to eventually resent doing it, whatever the "it" is, then don't.

SELF-CARE PRINCIPLE: The power of choice

Oh, I can hear you now, "Marion, you don't get it. I *have to* help him. He's desperate. I *have to* do this. I have *no* choice. You *have to* understand." No, actually, I don't. I may choose to understand, I may want to understand, it may behoove me to understand, but no one *has to* understand. Actually, no one *has to* do anything, and that includes you.

You don't "have to" anything

I recently posted on Facebook asking my friends what they did to celebrate Canada Day. One friend, who I love to the moon and back, posted, "I had to work." How often we all say we "have to" something.

I thought to myself that her choice of words provides insight into her thinking. "I had to work" sounds like being trapped, forced, and having no alternatives, whereas someone might argue that her options abound. This woman is retired and has always had a huge work ethic. She is employed as a seasonal worker and uses the income to fund her and her retired husband's annual vacations. They travel to Europe, take cruises, and enjoy their timeshare throughout North America several weeks per year. They love doing it and have earned every minute of that enjoyment. No one gave it to them. They both worked hard at their jobs and chose to responsibly plan financially for this phase of their lives.

> "The language you use speaks volumes of your underlying thinking".
> ~Marion Grobb Finkelstein

Here's the important thing to note: She's not working because she has to—she works because she chooses to do so and earn the benefits that this decision provides. She has many reasons for keeping this job, none of which includes that she has to. Has to, or what? What happens if she doesn't work? Does her world come to an end? Is her life over? Is her health compromised? Not at all. She bears the seasonal hours, sore muscles, and grouchy customers because she considers these inconveniences worth the benefits. She lives in a world of choice. See the difference?

The language you use speaks volumes of your underlying thinking. Check yours. Are you saying you "have to" when saying "want to", "going to", "will" or "choose to" would suffice? Your language is empowering when you are aware and conscious of the words you select. I invite you to notice how often you and others say "have to". When you find yourself using it, don't scold yourself--congratulate yourself that you noticed! Awareness is the first step toward changing the behaviour.

You have the gift of *choice*. With that comes a heady responsibility of making good choices (we'll be talking a lot more about that in the next chapter). You might not like that fact because it feels uncomfortable to know you're in the place and situation you are due, in large part, to your choices.

I'm not assigning blame or judgment and I don't want you to do that either. I encourage you to take a look at your life and examine the critical decisions you've made that contribute to you being where you are at this moment. Now think about all your daily self-talk and choices that hold you there. What are you telling yourself that keeps you planted in that place?

When it comes to choice, the options aren't all easy, though they always do exist. You likely have very valid reasons for not selecting many of them. Clearly, the cons of certain possibilities outweigh the benefits and that's why you shy away from selecting those. Although your chosen option may be difficult, somewhere in your decision-making process you have consciously or unconsciously determined that the path you will take is ultimately less painful than others or yields such rewards, it's worth the pain. Self-care means using empowering language and taking the path that leads to where you want to go. And you chose them.

Consider the case of Jennifer.

Jennifer feels judged

Jennifer adamantly disagrees with the way her friend's father-in-law routinely talks about large groups of people and how he makes sweeping and negative judgments. He professes to be a steadfast churchgoing Christian, yet uses racial slurs with complete disregard to how they hurt. He begins to tell Jennifer about some chairs that he recently got refinished, and proudly celebrates his negotiating skills by announcing that he "jewed down" his supplier.

Though Jennifer is appalled, she somehow manages to contain her expressions such that her face doesn't reveal her true disgust. Jennifer's husband is Jewish and she is mortified by this comment that feels somewhat like a personal attack, although she realizes it's not. She understands this man isn't targeting her or her husband specifically: He's painting a whole race with his one remark and her husband and family are coloured by his brush. Jennifer has heard of this expression but has never been in the presence of one so ignorant to use it as part of their common vernacular. Perhaps it was the father-in-law's oblivious attitude of how insulting he had just been that bothered her the most. She opts to believe he is blessedly unaware of his offensive choice of words because the alternative of him knowing and using them anyhow is beyond comprehension. She tells herself that, surely, even he isn't that rude and hurtful.

At that moment, Jennifer has a choice. She could speak up or choose to remain silent. For a list of reasons, she chooses the former. Turning to her friend's father, she replies calmly, "You jewed him down?", she begins. He nods yes. She continues, "May I remind you that Jesus Christ himself was born a Jew." For a fraction of a heartbeat, it seems he's taken off balance and at a loss for words. Satisfied that she's said her piece and pushed back to the extent *she feels comfortable, Jennifer turns on her heel and walks away leaving behind a perplexed father-in-law in her wake.*

Jennifer finds solace in knowing she'd had her say and concludes this man is too insensitive to even realize he had been challenged. She knows she runs the risk that her friend may not appreciate her push-back and is delighted, relieved, and surprised to discover not only is her friend grateful someone has finally put her father-in-law in his place, she also laughs at the spectacle of him standing there, slack-jawed and speechless. Jennifer chooses the behaviour; she chooses the consequences.

> "Indecision is a decision"
> ~Marion Grobb Finkelstein

Likewise, every time you choose to speak up or walk away, you also choose the consequences. Self-care is knowing which of these options best takes care of you and your interests.

In the example of Jennifer, you might not agree with her behaviour. You may be screaming silently, "Walk away! Don't waste your energy saying anything", yet Jennifer has her own reasons for choosing to speak up. She recognizes that even though others may think she has little choice but to leave silently, she's the one who makes that decision.

Likewise, inactivity--taking no action at all--is, in fact, a choice. Indecision *is* a decision. Ironically, being passive *is* an active choice in that you select that behaviour over the other options. The skill is in being aware that you are in fact *choosing* this path whether you do it consciously or by default. Acknowledging that you *choose* the best option for you at the time--given your skills, your knowledge, and your coping abilities--empowers you. This is the thinking of self-care.

How to decide to speak up or step away

The example about Jennifer raises a question I am often asked. That is, when is it best to speak up or step away? Self-care means making decisions that take care of you and your objectives. This includes preserving meaningful relationships and determining if stepping away or speaking up best serves your goals.

If you step away

When deciding to step away or not, consider the *possibility* of a negative outcome. Imagine the absolute worst case scenario if you step away and remain silent. Think about the worst result in a situation where you say nothing and it goes completely off the rails. Once you've done that, now assess the *probability* of that eventuality coming to pass. Yes, it may be possible but how *likely* is it to happen?

Now consider the ideal best outcome *possibility* should you step away. What's the *probability* of that happening? Yes, it's possible. How likely is it to happen that way?

When you assess the outcome of stepping away and saying nothing to likely be negative, you may no longer choose to remain silent and opt to speak up. On the other hand, when you believe that the probability of stepping away is most probably positive, that might be the option you choose.

A caution ...

If you consistently default to inaction, saying nothing, and avoiding confrontation, ask yourself if your needs are being met in doing so, or are you often feeling overlooked?

You deserve to be heard, to have your perspective considered, and for others to understand the impact of their actions, be they positive or negative. You have a right to consider the pros and cons of telling that person when their words cut through you or their actions sting. Perhaps you just need a little time to process and assess your response, but even with that, are hesitant to share it. Make sure that you don't compromise these rights in favour of your need to keep the peace and not make waves.

Make sure if you decide to step away, that it's for the right reasons and that your decision is best serving your goals and not simply appeasing your fears.

If you speak up

Now consider if you speak up, what would be the best *possible* outcome you could imagine? Now, look at the *probability* of that actually happening. If you think the likelihood is very good for a positive result, you may choose to take action and speak out in response. The operative word is "choose". You decide the action and in doing so, you choose the outcome.

Alternately, if you tend to speak your mind immediately without full consideration of the impact and consequences, does that best serve you? There is definitely a time and place for spontaneous and quick responses. Many people wish they had the gift of quick and snappy retorts. If you are gifted with this ability, know that this is an enviable strength. Like any tool, however, it may be used to help or harm.

The caution for you is to ensure that your fast response is moving you toward the end goal you want, and isn't something you will later regret.

The right choice is the one that works best for you

In the example above, to Jennifer, the option of remaining tight-lipped doesn't seem viable or worth the effort. If she says nothing, she really doesn't believe she is engaging in self-care in remaining silent as her value system is being attacked. She quickly evaluates, considers the options and likelihood of best case, worst case results, and determines that speaking up is what serves her. She is willing to run the risk of making waves and potentially upsetting her friend or her friend's father-in-law. She's quite comfortable with the possibility of the the father-in-law being angry with her, and is confident that her friendship with her bestie will withstand this unlikely upset. For Jennifer, it would be more painful to remain silent than to speak up. For her, this is the right choice.

Regardless of your natural communication preferences, you will either move toward pleasure and the result you want, or move away from pain and the result you fear.

Caution: Avoiding pain can be a powerful motivator--be cautious not to let that blind and stop you reaching for the possible rewards.

SELF-CARE CAUTION: Unmet needs will exist until they're met

Be aware that your unmet needs are forever simmering in the background. If they aren't satisfied or managed effectively, somehow, somewhere, they will bubble over and manifest themselves.

Ignoring your own needs doesn't make them disappear--it can make you bitter. It may set you up for a life of regret. This being said, know that you can change your goals. That's different than forgetting them and deceiving yourself into believing you can live without actualizing yourself.

Instead of giving up on your goals, you can figure out another way to reach them. Ask yourself why you want that goal, what is it you hope to gain? Once you know the "why", you'll figure out the how. Your goal may not manifest itself in the way you originally imagined, but you will look beyond this vision to meet your needs through different means.

If the same need keeps raising its head time and time again in your life, listen to it. Your truth is speaking. Your future is calling you to actualize yourself and be your best you.

When you satisfy your own needs, you blossom and develop your gifts. Meeting your own needs allows you to grow into the person you are meant to be--and that fulfilled and gifted person is the one the world desperately needs.

SELF-CARE PRINCIPLE: If you don't take care of yourself, someone else might

What I'm about to say comes from the place of tough love. I care deeply about helping you acquire the skills and assume the mindset and perspective that will best serve you. In that spirit, I'm going to be candid and direct as I share what I believe to be truths that have taken me a lifetime to learn. The bottom line is if you don't take care of yourself, you and others pay the consequence. It's time to put yourself on the agenda. Here's a few reasons why.

You may become a burden to others

If you give until you bleed, you may be setting yourself up to be a burden to others. This is the hard fact: When you chronically avoid self-care, you become a critical case requiring triage.

You can't survive and thrive if you're hemorrhaging finances, emotions, health, or any other vital part of your life. You run the dance of becoming a burden, a liability, or a risk to the very people who care about you. These people want to see you succeed and do well, and the last thing you want is to inconvenience them. However, when you put yourself in harm's way, even if to help someone else, it hurts to witness you struggling.

The message is clear: Take care of yourself so someone else doesn't have to.

Others may make decisions you wouldn't

When you don't engage in self-care, you may be surrender your decision-making power as others step in to handle what they see as a crisis. With the best of intentions and coming from a place of love and support--or in the worst case, from a place of abuse or opportunity--they may make decisions on your behalf that you would never make for yourself.

In short, if you don't take care of yourself, you could be surrendering your independence.

Those points might hurt to hear. Perhaps they touch a nerve and if they do, good. That means there's a degree of truth in it for you. Think about it for a moment. If you don't wrestle your own challenges to the ground, someone else--likely someone who loves you deeply--will feel obliged to step in and clean up the mess. It's too disturbing for them to see you in agony, even if it's of your own doing. When someone who loves you sees you drowning, he or she will only stand by so long watching you gasping for air before throwing you a lifesaver, perhaps at his or her own great personal risk.

Understand when you're being swallowed by your problems,

you are asking others around you to bear silent witness to your destruction and self-defeating actions. You are placing them in the unenviable position of wanting to do anything to end your discomfort and theirs of watching you writhe in discomfort. They may feel that if they help, they're enabling your behaviour and subjecting themselves to the subsequent guilt for doing so. Or they feel guilty for not helping. Either way, you are creating misery for those who truly care for you. No one who feels for you wants to see you suffer. Don't let them. Pull up your socks and manage your mess.

Engaging in self-care spares you from placing yourself or others in precarious situations.

Unheeded weather warnings

If you live in an area prone to hurricanes, tornadoes, forest fires, mudslides, and other weather-related disasters, you're familiar with the stern weather warnings issued from time to time. With today's technology, weather forecasters are able to predict impending severe weather conditions with increasing accuracy. In the most extreme cases, you have likely seen broadcasters and political figures pleading with residents to evacuate.

Almost without exception during these disasters, there is a handful of people who refuse to leave their homesteads, believing they can ward off whatever misfortunes come their way. Inevitably, these people get trapped and find themselves in life-threatening positions. The result? Brave first-responders are put in the dangerous position of risking their own lives to save those people who failed to heed the multiple evacuation warnings. Sometimes the resident perishes, in spite of all efforts. Other times, it's the first-responders who pay the ultimate price. In worse case scenarios, it's both.

All that risk and danger is so easily be avoided if these residents take proper care and evacuate when advised to do so by the experts. For whatever reason, they don't. It could be that they don't recognize the negative side effects from lack of self-care.

Now, think about your own life. What decisions have you made that negatively affect others? You may have many reasons for choosing the path you walk. If one of them is that you don't take care for yourself as well as you would someone else, revisit that thinking. Now that you understand the potential impact, it's time to self-care a little more.

The following example of reaching into your own pocket to help someone financially may hit home.

Fred's financial fiasco

Fred is a father and single parent of three adult children. He has instilled in his daughter and both his sons, a tremendous work ethic. Unfortunately, this is also coupled with Fred enabling his children's financial illiteracy.

Over the years, Fred works two jobs to pay for his children's post-secondary education and continues the support years after graduation. One of his sons lands a steady job, while the other and his daughter drift for several years, still living at home. During this time, Fred assumes all expenses. He justifies this action by telling himself that neither adult child has found their ideal job, and has no source of income.

A few years later, his daughter is married with two kids of her own. The marriage breaks down and she moves back in with her father and brother who is still there, and still unemployed. Although both his daughter and son hold down minimum wage jobs, neither has decent credit rating. Fred, thinking he is helping, co-signs for both to have lines of credit as his son buys a brand new car, while his daughter gets furniture and her own apartment.

Both these adult children are living well beyond their means. Their money management skills have been stunted as their father has traditionally paid for so much. Sadly, Fred doesn't acknowledge the negative effect of his crippling actions on his children's ability--or inability--to manage debt. He believes he's coming from a place of love and support.

Amplifying the dire circumstances, Fred and his two debt-challenged adult children increasingly become a source of worry to their friends and family. It's anguish for those who care for all of them to watch Fred struggling when it is clear his son and daughter are gloriously oblivious to the havoc they unknowingly create for the very person who loves them beyond words.

With his son and daughter barely cognizant there's a problem, Fred continues to enable their reckless spending and throws himself at the bottom of the care list, doing nothing to safeguard his own financial security and retirement years. Struggling to pay the bills and retain good credit rating, this father assumes all their line of credit debt and remortgages his house—twice.

Fred finally has a tell-all with his son and daughter and explains how this financial situation is crushing him. They are shocked, as they've never been told any of this over the years. Both quickly step up to assume responsibility and resign themselves to accepting less than dream jobs, and commit to years of working long hours to pay back their debts as quickly as possible. Eventually, they bite into the mound of bills they've each helped create, and allow their father a sigh of relief in his senior years.

What's the moral? In his effort to support his children, Fred *jeopardizes his own future. Fred and his daughter and one son have forgotten one of the principles of self-care: If you don't take care of yourself, someone else inherits your mess. Fred, his son, and daughter, put themselves and each other in financial danger and under unbearable stress. The good news? They communicated honestly with each other, assumed responsibility, and got the lesson of self-care before it was too late.*

SELF-CARE ACID TEST: Are you crippling someone else's opportunity to learn life skills?

In addition to the danger of passing your problems to someone else, Fred's story demonstrates another self-care principle--don't rob someone else of the chance to learn a life skill. Step back, let them fall. Don't always catch your loved one. That's how people learn. There is no failure, just feedback. Falling down isn't important--getting back up is what counts. So them them fall: That's how they learn to stand on their own.

Are you robbing someone of a valuable learning lesson? If the answer is "yes", even though you may be motivated by care and support, you may not be manifesting it in the most productive way. Instead, your lack of self-care, your action of putting yourself at unnecessary risk and of doing everything for this other person, may be counterproductive and not serving you or the other at all.

SELF-CARE PRINCIPLE: You can't give what you don't have.

Getting what you need is a healthy approach to life that keeps you energized and fulfilled. Expressing your needs and what you want is a big part of building healthy self-esteem and confidence.

On the note of getting your needs met, there is a field of mounting research suggesting a link between chronic illness and the inability to productively express your own needs.

In his 2012 book, *When the Body Says No (The Cost of Hidden Stress)*[1], Canadian medical doctor, Gabor Maté, cites many studies indicating a relationship between unexpressed emotions of anger and resentment--even if they are subconscious--being a trigger for chronic illnesses including cancer, Alzheimer's, and immunology disorders such as rheumatoid arthritis and scleroderma. After sometimes a lifetime of ignoring signals and getting mixed messages that you don't count, your body finally responds and starts attacking itself. Then, you pay for the chronic stress your lack of self-care has dished out to your body for years. (Of course, there are genetic factors involved too. I believe the lack of self-care simply acts as a trigger).

Imagine a world where you love yourself as much as you love others, where you care for yourself as much as you do them. Forget about that misguided sense of loyalty to others who haven't earned it and that always comes at a cost to yourself. That underlying thinking is trapping you in a losing cycle.

SELF-CARE PRINCIPLE: You're worth it

Are you avoiding self-care because there's a little, tiny piece of yourself that believes you're not worth it? Maybe you're holding yourself back and thinking that someone else more deserving has earned your time and resources. Perhaps some life event or person has imprinted you with the incorrect lesson that you're not worthy of attention. Let me assure you--you *are*!

If any of what I just said resonates with you, let me shake up that underlying belief. The fact that you exist, that you're reading this message right now, that you give so much to so many, all point to the fact that you are more than worthy to receive self-care.

How you care for yourself tells the world how much you value your own being. Further, it models for others how to treat you. You *are* worthy. You *have* earned it. You *deserve* to take time and care for yourself. If anyone tells you otherwise, consider the source--it just might be someone who resents you not spending every second with him or her. It might mean you're introducing change to your current relationships and not everyone is going to like that.

You deserve to treat yourself well. If you don't believe this in every fibre of your being, no one else will either.

EXERCISE: Identify what you really need (and have been missing)

Knowing where to focus your efforts to get the best results can be daunting. The universe is sending you messages, you just need to know how to decode them. These following exercises will help you do exactly that.

Wands and wishes

Right now, I want you to dream a little. If I handed you a magic wand and said you have as many wishes as you need to be happy, what would you wish? In other words, what aspects of your life would you love to change?

My colleague, Roxanne Derhodge, a certified psychotherapist in the Niagara region, offers another insightful question she puts to her many clients to unearth areas of their life that need attention.

Play along here and see how you answer.

Imagine you have just awakened to wonderful news: A miracle has happened in your life! It's something amazing that will change everything for you. Live in that moment, feel it, breathe it, experience it. And now, the salient question: What was it that jumped into your mind?

How you answer reveals a troubling sore spot in your life, likely one that is draining you in some way. It often is this bothersome area that requires the greatest attention. Maybe you can change it. Maybe you can't. Even if you're not able to change the circumstance or person involved, you most certainly can choose to change your response.

Whether you chose the wand or the miracle, what answer bubbled up to the surface for you? Don't overthink it. Go with your gut responses. If you didn't do the exercise as you were reading, take a moment now and let your mind wander. The answer is there. You already know what aspects of your life require energy and are sucking you dry. You just need the right questions for them to reveal themselves and become consciously aware. These questions will help. If nothing surfaces immediately, ask them just before you go to sleep and see how you answer in the morning. Your subconscious will work away as you dream to help you respond.

Rate your satisfaction

Here's another exercise that will help you focus in on the pieces of your life requiring attention and a little more self-care. Grab a piece of paper or mentally go through and rate your degree of satisfaction in each life area in the list I'm going to give you in a moment. Be honest and go with your first gut response. No one is going to see these answers except you. This isn't a pass or fail test. This is simply an indicator that will help you move forward.

As you're rating your degree of satisfaction, keep in mind your own definitions of "success". For example, if you don't make what others would consider a lot of money and you figure you don't really need or want more than you currently have, then you may rate your satisfaction on that factor as quite high. You're completely comfortable with the status quo. Others may rate your situation differently, and that doesn't matter. This is *your* satisfaction rating, per *your* definitions of what *you* want, not someone else.

As a side-note, if other people's opinion of you weighs more heavily than your own personal opinion, if you're hanging with people who consistently leave you feeling inferior, maybe one of the changes you'll want to consider changing is your circle of friends.

Now, let's get to it. On a scale of 1 being low and 10 being high, indicate how satisfied you are with these aspects of your life:

- Work/career
- Health / Physical
- Social/community
- Friends
- Family / Significant other
- Financial
- Spiritual
- Self-esteem and confidence
- Overall happiness

There have been two points in my career, many years apart, where I experienced bully bosses. During both those periods, I felt out of balance and didn't know quite where to turn for help. This exercise gave me direction and suggested where my efforts would be best spent. It helped me to triage my life. At that time of crisis, my chart would have looked something like this:

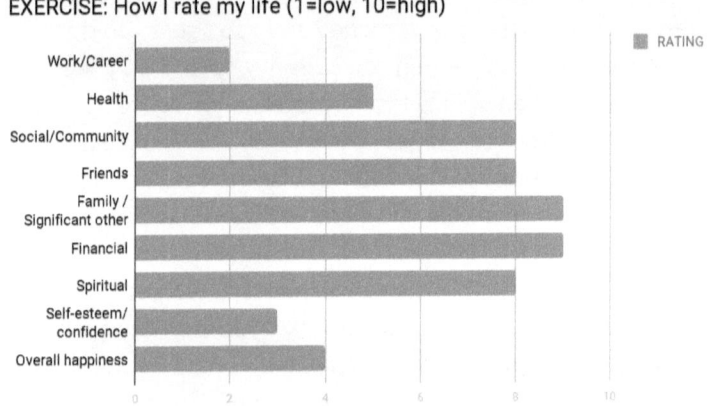

EXERCISE: How I rate my life (1=low, 10=high)

During this trying episode, it's evident from the high ratings I assigned that I had a strong network of supportive friends, family, and community. The low scores are also very telling. The career aspect of my life during this bully time was rated exceptionally low and, as a result, was impacting negatively on my self-esteem and overall happiness.

When I unpacked the work situation, I realized that I loved my actual job and duties and adored my colleagues--it was the unpredictable and nasty nature of the boss that was sucking the fun out of everything I had previously enjoyed. His communication and leadership styles were the problem. The effects of his toxic behaviour were damaging me and his other direct reports. We were all paying a huge emotional toll that was beginning to manifest itself in my physical symptoms such as lack of sleep, appetite, and energy.

This chart exercise allowed me to step back and examine my situation logically. It enabled me to remove the intense emotion I felt and to precisely identify where my efforts and limited energy would have the greatest impact on achieving my desired outcome. It provided the framework for my action plan which you will hear more about in later chapters.

Now take a look at *your* scores. What did you rate as an 8, 9 or 10? Those are the pieces of your life where you're rocking it. Bravo! Take a moment to breathe that in and commend yourself. Those are the areas where you might be able to help others, to be a resource, and to share your expertise with those who want to grow. Congratulations. Those are some of your gifts you can use to help others.

Next, ask what is it you are doing in these high-scoring areas of your life that is making you feel so satisfied? Celebrate those skills and strategies you've mastered, and apply those very approaches and processes to other areas that you rated as low and require improvement. Those strategies may well work there too.

Now for the aspects where you rated medium scores of 5 to 7. These are areas where you ideally would like to improve and it seems well within your reach to do so. You're already on your way, so give it more attention and effort and chances are that your ratings here will improve.

It's the low-ranking aspects, those that you rated as a scant 1 to 4, that require your attention. These are your growth opportunities and where you desperately need self-care. Assuming that these areas are important to you, this is where you will want to set boundaries and invest energy. These are the aspects of your life that aren't very satisfying for you right now. You can change that.

Be gentle with yourself. Don't for a second chide yourself for not being more of whatever it is you wish you were. As much as you are encouraging and nurturing to others, be so with yourself. Learning to self-care when you've had a life of caring for others is difficult. It takes time to master this new set of self-care skills. It requires examining your motivations and self-talk.

Remember to be kind in the language you use with yourself. That's part of self-care. How you talk to yourself has a huge impact on how you think, behave, and how others perceive you.

It's very revealing to think about a time when you messed up and were super stressed, and remember what you said to yourself. Were you kind or did you cuss yourself out? Does your self-talk self-sabotage? Are you typically far harder on yourself than you ever would be with another person? Does the little insecure kid inside you begin shouting at your inner self? I had a taste of that the other day.

My mid-life memory and self-talk

My husband, Steve, is a professional musician. One of the several bands he plays in was giving a summer concert in a local park and friends were meeting us there for the show. No sooner had we driven around the corner from our place than I realize I'd forgotten my cell phone.

Immediately, I start playing it out in my mind: How would I text my friends to tell them where I was sitting so we could find each other? How could I take pictures and video I could post on social media? And it began--the self-talk. I roll my eyes, audibly sigh, and silently chide my forgetfulness. Better I tell my husband so we could turn around than I get there with no cell phone. I apologetically explain the situation and Steve, a.k.a., "Mr. Punctuality" who is in a rush to get there for band set-up, turns the beast around and we pull back into our driveway. I run in, grab the phone and dash back out.

We just turn around the same first corner again when I realize I'd forgotten my little stool to sit on. We were told that the park had no benches and this was a BYOC—bring your own chair—event. With a deep sigh of exasperation and unbridled disgust, I exclaim, "Oh geez, I forgot my stool". I don't have to look at Steve's face--I know what his expression is. I refuse his stilted offer to turn around for a second time, knowing his anxiety level is already through the roof. So is mine.

At that very moment, there is nothing Steve could think or say to me that I am not thinking or saying to myself. As he drives, I console myself with the option of sitting on my jacket that I caustically tell myself I somehow managed to remember. When we arrive at the venue, I immediately find a vacant picnic table and quickly claim it as my own. All my concerns were unfounded. So was my initial act of chastising myself.

Can you relate? I'm guessing that you've been there too, whipping yourself unnecessarily. If you self-deprecate on a regular basis, you're undermining yourself and your goals. Love yourself a little bit more.

Now that you acknowledge the behaviour, even if you do it only sometimes, you're in a better position to change it. This is exactly what you'll be exploring in the following chapters.

Awareness is the first step. If the behaviour isn't serving you well, change it. You deserve to be supported in your efforts, and that begins with you supporting yourself with kind self-talk.

SELF-CARE PRINCIPLE: Love isn't limited.

Loving yourself as much as you love others doesn't take more energy--it gives it. If self-care isn't part of your daily routine, you are ripe pickings for the energy vampires in your life. They will circle around and suck you dry if you let them. Don't you dare let them!

In her book, *Dodging Energy Vampires*, medical doctor Christiane Northrup reminds us, "When we dim our light to make others feel more comfortable, the whole world gets darker".[2] She encourages us to do the opposite and shine ever brighter.

Love doesn't come in limited quantities. If you're a parent, then you know as each child is born or brought into your family through other means, you don't stop loving the next one just because you already have a child or have several. Not at all. Your heart expands to include the new addition. Your love multiplies. So too with self-love.

Giving yourself some love doesn't mean you have less to give others. Quite the opposite. Self-care allows you to give far more than you ever thought possible. It gives you the ability to live in a world of abundance versus scarcity, or as some would call it, "scare city". Love isn't limited, it spreads and grows to encompass all the people in your circle, and that includes you.

Love yourself as much as you love others. Your heart has room and is waiting to welcome you.

Discover why self-care scares you

It's useful for you to figure out what is holding you back from self-care. You assume various roles in your family, friendships, and workplace. Are you the one who normally takes care of others, the one all colleagues come to when in need? Are you the glue in the family that holds everyone together?

If you think your role is crucial to all these relationships and group dynamics, give your head a shake. The reality is that the universe isn't going to fall apart and will adapt quite well if you pull back your generosity just a little bit from others and turn it a little more toward yourself.

There's a little (or maybe a lot) of ego tied up in being a saviour or thinking your role is critical to others.

I don't believe there's truly any such thing as "altruism", giving without getting anything back. You might not get traditional payment, though you always get back something when you give to others: You get that feel-good feeling, however fleeting. You get that feeling inside that you make a difference because you really do. When you give of yourself, you have an impact. You get to hone your skills in whatever it is you're giving. If it's cooking up a meal, you're heralded as a great cook and wonderful hostess. If it's fixing a neighbour's car, you're applauded for being a fantastic mechanic. If you lend a listening ear even when you're exhausted, you earn a reputation for being patient and kind and you gain insights to others' lives. Those are rewards. It feels good to be able to help, and yes, there's a pinch of ego and superiority in that feeling too. Those are rewards.

What rewards are you afraid of losing if you engage in more self-care instead of giving so much to support others? The following acid tests will assist you in deciding if it's time to take care of yourself just a little bit more.

SELF-CARE ACID TEST: Three tests to measure your degree of self-care and decide if it's time for more

Sometimes it's difficult to know if giving to someone else is the right thing to do or not. Is it best for you and the other person if you walk away and let them learn on their own? Or will lending a helping hand help them or you grow further?

Considering the other person's perspective is important. Equally so, it's vital in good decision-making to consider your own perspective. I've often struggled with knowing if stepping in to help or rescue is loving or enabling. That's a question you alone can ask and answer for your specific situation.

When I present workshops, I share what I call, "acid tests" you can use at litmus tests to check your decision-making directions. Here's a few tests you can give yourself to see if it's time to step up and give, or if it's the right occasion for you to step away and allow for some much-needed self-care and downtime.

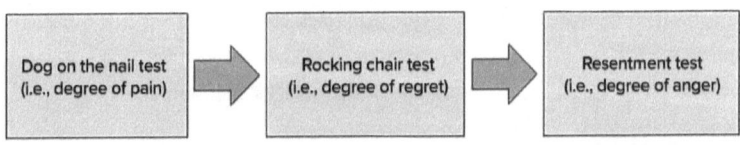

- Dog on the nail test. There is a man sitting cross-legged on the street with his dog curled up beside him. Along comes another fellow who looks down and asks the seated man, "Excuse me, sir. I notice your dog keeps getting up, turning around and sitting back down. Why? What's he doing?" The seated man replies, "Well, he's sitting on a nail and every now and then gets up to change position." The passerby is astonished by this response and asks, "If he's sitting on a nail, why doesn't he just move?", to which the dog-owner explains, "Because it doesn't hurt enough." Ahhh ... it doesn't hurt enough for him to actually move. So let me ask you this: Does your lack of self-care affect you so negatively that you ache to change your reality? Is your lack of self-care hurting so much that you are motivated to change your situation? If the answer is yes, then pull back on the giving. You've earned the right to set boundaries, stop the pain, and bump up the self-care.

- Rocking chair test. Think about the self-care you give yourself right now. Take a snapshot of how it looks. Now fast-forward to the point that you're in a rocking chair with your life behind you and only a few days left in front. As you rock, your life passes before your eyes and you see that photo of the amount of self-care you gave yourself. Does it make you feel good? Are you proud of how you treated yourself? Or does it make you feel sad and regretful? Do you wish you'd given yourself more chances, invested more time and energy in yourself? If you had it to live all over again, would you care for yourself more? If the answer is yes, take hope! You still have time. Zoom back to current day and view it from the perspective as if you were in the future and looking back. Doing so will add clarity to your decision of whether you need more self-care or not. If you will regret your lack of self-care, change that now.

- Resentment test. Do you or will you resent it if you give more to others and less to yourself? This question is the quintessential acid test one. If someone is beseeching upon your good nature for a favour, if you're wondering if you should or shouldn't, if you don't know if doing so will compromise your self-care, ask yourself if you do what he or she is asking, will you regret it? Or are you already doing it and a piece of you, no matter how small or buried, feels angry and put out about it. Get in touch with your real and authentic feelings. Allow yourself to be human. It's okay. In fact, there is great wisdom in knowing that it's worse to do something and then harbour a deep resentment than to not do it at all. This is true even if your anger is deeply hidden, unconscious, and you weren't aware of how you really felt until this very moment. The act of setting boundaries is healthy and this one question will guide you in doing so.

I've used these questions myself for tough life predicaments. Asking these acid test questions guides me through many difficult situations where I struggle to decide if stepping in is a loving thing to do for me and the other person or persons, or if self-care is more about setting boundaries. These questions have helped me immeasurably and have helped hundreds, perhaps thousands, of my clients over the years.

You show what you value by how you spend your resources. Let that sink in for a moment. Where and how are *you* spending *your* resources?

When you demonstrate through actions that you value yourself, others will follow your lead. No one will value you until you value yourself. Giving yourself love, time, and respect isn't vanity or selfishness. Rather, self-care gives others an opportunity to be proud of yourself and your worthy accomplishments. Self-care reflects in how you groom yourself, talk to and about yourself, and treat yourself.

> You show what you value by how you spend your resources".
> ~Marion Grobb Finkelstein

You show others how to treat you by how you treat yourself. The world needs you and you deserve--correction--you *owe* it to yourself and others to be able to play at one hundred percent capacity.

Self-care makes sense for so many reasons and none of them are selfish. The message is clear: Speak your truth. Draw boundaries and get yourself on the agenda. Do it to help yourself. Do it to help others grow. Do it for the health of it.

Chapter 2 recap

You've covered a lot of territory in this chapter and built an amazing foundation to support everything you're about to learn in the coming chapters. Let's review to refresh your memory of the key points:

- Avoid the victim mindset;
- If healthcare professionals could help you, get them and let them;
- Don't give until it hurts, just give until it feels good;
- You have the power of choice;
- If you don't take care of yourself, someone else may--your problem becomes theirs; their decisions become yours;
- You can't give what you don't have (keep your cup full);
- Love isn't limited so love yourself as much as you do others;
- Don't let fear hold you back from self-care you deserve;
- Use the acid test questions to measure your degree of self-care;

- You show the world what you value by how you spend your resources--spend some on yourself with self-care.

In the next chapter, we begin the real work of dealing with situations that go wrong. You'll break it down into several actionable steps and I'll help you walk through each. The first one begins with defining the loss. Let me show you how.

---

[1] Gabor Maté, When the Body Says No (The Cost of Hidden Stress), Big Happy Family, LLC, Post Hypnotic Press Inc., 2012
[2] Christiane Northrup, Dodging Energy Vampires, Hay House Inc., USA, 2018, pg.146

CHAPTER 3

STEP 1: ACKNOWLEDGE YOUR LOSS
What's your problem?

Now we're ready to get into the nitty gritty of moving forward and we're going to do it with a series of steps, each one giving cause for pause and reflection. I've broken down my system into three steps as follows:

> STEP 1: Acknowledge your loss
> STEP 2: Four flippin' questions
> STEP 3: Let go

You might be tempted to skip over this first step and jump right into the four questions of the *Flip It Formula*™, that will help you flip your negative situation into a positive outcome. I strongly encourage you to resist that temptation. Whether you're grappling with your own losses or want to better understand someone else living through a thorny situation, take the time to invest in this critical first step. You will reap the rewards multifold and you will then be fully prepared to move to the other steps and squeeze out every drop of benefit they hold.

ACKNOWLEDGE YOUR LOSS

LOSS PRINCIPLE: Your situation robs you of your goals

Think about your specific challenge. Whatever difficulty you're wrestling to the ground, it's taking you away from your goals.

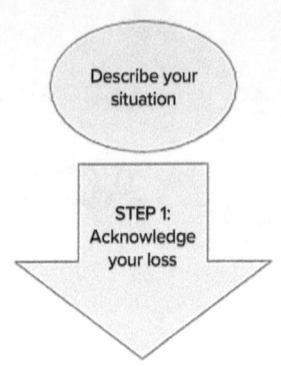

Write it down. Describe what is getting under your skin in factual terms. Explain it as if you were a third-person looking in on your situation, an impartial bystander. Pretend you're preparing a legal brief or concise executive summary. Remove yourself from the emotion of the situation and view it objectively. Imagine yourself being a hardcore news reporter.
No judgement. Just the facts, ma'am, just the facts.

Once you have a clear idea about, and are able to succinctly describe your specific situation in factual terms, you're ready to graduate to the first step in the Finkelstein Factor™ process. Warning: It's a tricky one.

It's time now to acknowledge your loss.

In other words, what is your difficult situation or challenge robbing you from doing, being, achieving, or experiencing? In this chapter, you will learn how to enunciate your hurt and put words around what is holding you stymied. Giving voice to the pain allows you to understand and release it.

Let's look at a the example of Tony giving eldercare, a circumstance that many people inherit.

Tony and his elderly Mom

As a child, Tony and his younger brother were close to their parents. Tony has a warm and loving mother-son relationship, punctuated with what one would arguably call the normal ebbs and flows of any child-parent interaction. When he is in his forties with a family and significant other, Tony's seventy-something mother is diagnosed with a brain tumour. In spite of a successful operation, the following decade brings with it ever-increasing physical and medical challenges. The trauma to the brain results in Tony's mother becoming more argumentative, stubborn, and difficult to reason with. Stumbles and falls are frequent occurrences and the latest blow is a stroke.

Tony's step-father, married to his mother for twenty-some years, refuses to arrange for Tony's mother to move to a permanent assisted-living home upon leaving the care facility in a few days. He cites finances and spousal obligation as reasons why he won't do it. Tony doesn't buy either reason and sees them not as explanations but as selfish excuses for denying his mother the care he feels she truly deserves. He has reason to believe that his mother and father-in-law could readily afford the medical assistance and that they are just too money-conscious to release the funds. He bites his tongue as he sees his mother slip further away from him emotionally, mentally, and physically. The impact of the stroke is settling in and leaves Tony's mother as a shell of her former self. Tony fears greatly that his mother being released to go home instead of a care facility is an unwise choice. It will result in a senior taking care of a senior and put his mother in a home with stairs and a cause to worry about dangerous falls.

Tony is in pain. He is short-tempered and angry at the world, at the unfairness of illness and disease, at witnessing his mother not getting the care he believes she has earned, and at his inability to control or influence the situation. He feels his concerns are falling consistently on deaf ears. His solely-owned business is taking a huge hit as he spends hours on end with daily hospital visits. He is no longer able to respond to client requests and to feed his sales funnel. The impact of this month or two on his business will take months, if not years, to undo. Having just purchased a new home, the financial pressures are tremendous. Tony is about to break.

In an effort to relieve Tony's load, his younger brother is phoning their mom daily for quick five-minute calls as that's the longest his mother can hold focus. Tony's brother is also a solopreneur. Unlike Tony, however, his brother's work schedule is heavy with travel commitments and he believes his being in town with Tony would do nothing to improve the situation, so he continues with business as usual and earning uninterrupted revenues.

Meanwhile, in the care facility, Tony's mother mulishly refuses the physical assistance offered from healthcare workers and family members. She snubs their efforts to help her holding the phone or initiating calls. Her brain injuries and now the stroke leave her finding it too overwhelming to watch television or listen to the radio. The option of using Skype or Facetime is explored and discarded as this medium is also beyond her capacity. The recent stroke and her obstinate behaviour complicate matters to the point that it leaves Tony's mother unable to do much more than pass the long hours staring at the walls and Tony swimming in unwarranted guilt. He has done nothing to create this situation and yet Tony feels he bears the lion's share of its weight upon his weary shoulders. He is the intown son, the one who is closest physically and not travelling, so believes it is his duty to oversee his mother's every need. He is exhausted and feels solely responsible to entertain and visit his mother daily to save her from her self-imposed sentence of solitude.

So what is Tony's loss? When he and I connected, I asked him that question. What was it that he was aching for, that was gone forever, and that he was unwillingly giving up? What was he mourning? Upon probing, Tony was able to define about twenty losses. Here's a sampling of just a few:

- Losing a parent, possibly physically, certainly emotionally and cognitively;
- Losing the pleasure of stimulating conversations they used to have;
- Losing a close mother-son relationship he never really had in adult years;
- Losing time previously spent on relaxing activities, now dedicated to elder care;
- Losing a sense of control and life balance;
- Losing other relationships because of time spent on this one;
- Losing respect for others who could be helping and aren't, getting resentful;
- Losing business clients and revenue;
- Losing sleep, health, and sense of well-being.

Do any of these losses sound familiar to you? Some of them may jump off the page and speak to you if you have lived a similar experience. If you read this list and feel a little twinge, if the situation or some of the losses listed resonate with you, this may help you to put words to *your* pain.

This is a demanding journey for Tony in the story above. He is having difficulty understanding the underlying emotion and admits that, as arduous as this task can be, enunciating these losses helps him manage by now understanding the source of the strong emotions he is feeling. Doing this exercise and acknowledging your loss, whatever it might be, will help you face, embrace, and replace your silent hurt with a voice.

LOSS PRINCIPLE: Life isn't controllable. Your responses are.

Whoever told you life is fair, lied. It's not justice, it just is. Bad things happen to good people. Not all the time, but sometimes. Not to all people, but to some. Hardworking individuals get passed over for promotions. Talented performers never catch that big break. Spouses cheat. Diseases hit. Finances crash.

The key is knowing how to respond when these things go wrong. The good news is that even though you don't control all the variables life rolls in your direction, the one thing you do control completely is how you respond.

When you face a difficult life challenge, you might be fine for a while and completely deceived into believing you can handle it full-time. Maybe it's not a major life-altering event and you manage to pass through it with grace. Then, a series of seemingly small events pile up, one after another and their impact is cumulative. Challenges and grief affect all of us differently and you can't predict with certainty how you will feel or react.

You can't control what life throws at you, but you can decide to throw it back or keep it. You control how you respond, and that fact empowers you.

EXAMPLE: Budget cuts

In the Finkelstein Factor™ workshops, a workplace situation that I often use as an example of a change you don't control, is budget cuts. Just about everyone in the workforce relates to this and for good reason. With economic pressures, political decisions, and requirements for highly skilled personnel these days, many businesses are looking for ways to earn more revenue and decrease costs, resulting in smaller assigned budgets. The end result can be demanding work conditions. Sometimes organizations cut back so much they're no longer cutting the fat--they're now chopping into the muscle. If you haven't lived this experience of what is coined as right-sizing, just wait. Chances are pretty good that at some point in your career, you'll taste this bitter pill and truly understand how difficult it can be to swallow.

Using this example of budget cuts, my workshop participants brainstorm many possible losses that budget cuts might present in their workplace. Some of these losses they have experienced or fear are listed below:

- *Loss of ability to complete projects as originally planned;*
- *Loss of bonuses;*
- *Loss of salary;*
- *Loss of staff;*
- *Loss of job security;*
- *Loss of workplace morale;*
- *Loss of employee engagement;*
- *Loss of employee loyalty;*
- *Loss of internal upward mobility;*
- *Loss of travel to visit clients;*
- *Loss of client relationships;*
- *Loss of sales;*
- *Loss of promotional efforts;*
- *Loss of market share;*
- *Loss of pride of working at the organization.*

These losses related to company budget cuts are provided for example purposes only. You could brainstorm a dozen others. There are no right, wrong, or perfect number of answers, just losses that make sense to you.

Once you get started with your list of losses you'll find that you can go off in various tangents. Surrender to the process. Let it lead you to losses you haven't yet acknowledged and explored. That's how you will become consciously aware of what's bothering you the most. The deeper you dig, the more effort you give, and the longer you stick with creating this list, the more likely you will uncover concerns and fears you never realized you had. When you do have such discoveries, don't dwell on them: Feel them and give yourself a pat on the back--revel in that aha moment. Success! You've defined your loss. And then move on.

LOSS PRINCIPLE: Admitting hurt is a strength

Some people may believe that admitting hurt is a sign of weakness. I believe quite to the contrary: It's an act of strength. It speaks of someone strong enough to face his or her fears, perhaps for the first time ever. Doing so is left to the formidable amongst us who have the chutzpah, courage and confidence. Experiencing hurt makes you human and relatable.

Admitting a loss doesn't make you a loser--it readies you to win.

LOSS PRINCIPLE: Acknowledging losses validates your pain

You feel the way you do for a reason, maybe many reasons. It is exceptionally validating to enunciate your losses because it helps you and others understand what you're going through. Acknowledging your losses offers explanation for your sadness, anger, or whatever emotion you find yourself experiencing as a result of your pain.

It also builds a bridge inside yourself between the hurt and the healing.

The following case study is difficult for me to share because it's my own. I'm ripping back the curtain of my private life to demonstrate how I personally have used and benefited from the practices I'm suggesting. I have shared this story from the platform when speaking at conferences and without fail, it is met with tears and hugs from attendees who have lived similar experiences. They thank me for enunciating what they have endured and lost, and I am only able to do this because of this process I'm now sharing with you. Regardless of the heartache you may be experiencing now, see if you relate to any of this sense of loss.

EXAMPLE: Marion's loss of a family dream

When I am in my teens, I can't wait to start babysitting. As a high school student, my summers are filled being a playground counsellor. Throughout university, I tutor kids in math. Having nieces and a nephew in three different cities, I travel several times a year in every season from Ottawa to North Bay and the Niagara Region to be an active part of their young lives. I love children and envision myself as being a mom with two, maybe three kids. Life has different plans.

Four miscarriages and a couple medical interventions later, nothing, no children. My husband and I explore the domestic adoption option and though we believe we have everything to offer--supportive families on both sides, a child-friendly home built and located with children in mind, steady jobs and financial security--and we enthusiastically note to the social worker doing the home study that we would welcome a child of any age, race, colour, or creed, even sibling pairs, we never receive one phone call about a match in four and a half years.

When I turn forty, it no celebration. I feel our window of opportunity is closed tight, in fact, nailed shut. My life has taken a twist I didn't expect. I begin to consider my losses and why I feel so depressed. My list is long and tear-stained. Here are a scant few of the highlights:

- *Loss of the motherhood experience I see my friends and colleagues enjoying;*
- *Loss of commonality with friends and relatives who have kids;*
- *Loss of every special occasion and milestone shared with a child;*
- *Loss of seeing my grown children graduate, marry, have kids;*
- *Loss of sharing our children with our parents (and loss of their joy);*
- *Loss of seeing what a great father my husband would have been;*
- *Loss of leaving a vestige of myself behind;*
- *Loss of sharing my life lessons;*
- *Loss of someone to love me, visit, and advocate for me when I'm a senior;*
- *Loss of identity and the person I thought I would be.*

A magic thing happens when, after my fourth miscarriage–I

decide to no longer silently suffer and tell some close colleagues really what is happening. Them knowing my loss helps them to understand and validate my sadness and this greatly helps me move through it.

Working through the exercise of defining losses helps me realize that this is why I do the work I do. Speaking at conferences and helping clients communicate better with themselves and others, is how I share my lessons, leave a vestige, and know that I make a difference in someone's life. I'm still reaching my goals and addressing my needs, just fulfilling them in different ways than I'd originally planned. Once you define your losses and understand the goals you were hoping to attain, you too can develop alternate ways to get what you need to feel fulfilled.

You may relate to some of these types of losses even if you do have children and especially if you don't, or if you know someone who has lived a similar experience. That's the interesting part: Some types of losses are universal regardless of the cause. However, if none of these items on my list of losses resonate with you, that's fine too. This is *my* list, just as your list will be solely yours. No one else needs to see it if you don't want them to do so.

Alternately, if you gain strength and solace from showing your list to a confidante or someone who cares, it goes miles toward your healing. It also helps them understand your perspective more clearly. Explaining your pain to other people, showing your vulnerable side, can build you support in unexpected places.

This exercise of defining my losses definitely helps me understand why I felt profoundly sad at that time: I was giving up a lot. It validates my heartbreak and gives me words to understand it myself and, if and when necessary, to explain it to others. It also provides me with the insight to be compassionate to others living a similar situation. In fact, I've had people thank me for putting into words what they were unable to. Defining your loss helps you and others understand why you feel and are reacting the way you do. Give it a try.

YOUR TURN: What is your loss?

In your situation, what is it that you believe you're losing and why does that scare you? What are you afraid of losing?

Your pain buttons and list of losses will include both actual happenings and potential events that worry you. Describe present-day realities as well as concerns you're afraid may manifest in future. No need to explain or justify your worries. They don't need to be founded or logical. If it bothers you, if you feel you're losing or will likely lose something, write it down. Avoid telling yourself that something on your list is foolish and shouldn't be there.
Of course it should be. If it's your loss, it's real, and it's causing you pain. Validate that voice inside of you. Let it be heard and commend yourself on admitting, perhaps for the first time, why you hurt.

Craft your list of losses

Don't stop at three or four items, keep your list growing. The more you write, the more you will realize. The more that bubbles to the top and the conscious level, the more you'll understand why this situation hurts so deeply. Some people fill pages once they get going because the floodgates are finally opened.

Here are some questions that will help get you going:

- PAST: What have you lost, conceded, given up that you are mourning?
- PRESENT: What scares you about the status quo and current situation?
- FUTURE: If this situation continues, what do you fear you'll lose in future?

As you work your way through listing your losses, you'll become aware of how deep your cut is and how very much it has injured you. You may find yourself getting angry as you confront through your hurts. Perhaps your reaction is profound sadness as you relive your dark moments. Maybe it is guilt for having spoken too fast before you thought it through, or regret for not speaking up and saying what you really thought. Whatever the emotion, go with it. You're getting in touch with your sensations and the real reason your situation holds a grip on you. The more difficult the situation, the more emotionally charged it's likely to be. If emotions erupt, it's because the loss is that deep. Let them.

If you don't actually write down your list of losses, at minimum think about them. If you have a confidante, someone you trust implicitly, talk it over with him or her. This person will add perspective and may be able to give you the words you lack. If you don't have such a person in your life, you still have yourself. You can most definitely do this exercise alone—most people do. Or if you'd prefer to discuss with the support of a group or coach, seek out those options (feel free to contact me Marion@MarionSpeaks.com).

This exercise of listing your losses is incredibly revealing. The more time and effort you spend defining your losses, the easier the following steps will be. When you're done, you will be in a better position to explain and understand why you were having difficulty managing and were stymied.

Yes, and then what?

As you grow your list of losses, keep asking why that loss hurts. Probe by exploring, "then what?" In the example of job loss, it's not just about losing money: It's about losing what money *provides*. Stay with the hurt and keep digging. Get into that headspace and really feel what it is you're giving up and losing. Delving further, you may unearth additional losses associated with money as being:

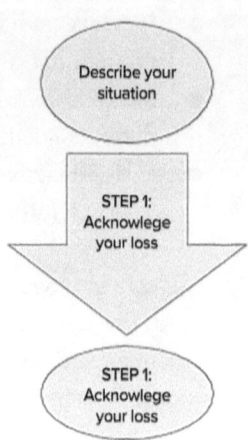

- Loss of prestige (then what?)
- Loss of pride and freedom (then what?)
- Loss of independence (then what?)
- Loss of options (then what?)
- Loss of joint vacations with friends (then what?)
- Loss of friendships (then what?)
- Loss of social circles and status (then what?)
- Loss of family (then what?)
- Loss of care and companionship in senior years (then what?) ...

The beauty of this process is that your list won't be like anyone else's. It will be tailored to you and your own fears, deep-rooted concerns, your experience, and your relationships. Who cares why you have those fears or if others would find them justified. For now, just acknowledge and accept them as yours. Don't challenge or doubt them, simply go with the process. These fears are as real for you as anything in your life. Drop the judgment. There are no right or wrong answers, just honest ones--just yours.

You may find after applying this exercise over and over again, as I hope you do, that patterns emerge and certain fears keep raising their heads. That's excellent! Now you know that these fears are your triggers. Now, you can begin to comprehend cognitively, on a conscious basis, why you tend to react so strongly and with a visceral response to certain stimuli—they're pushing your loss buttons! You will be able to appreciate these reactions as warning signs that it's time to address those needs or suffer those losses.

LOSS PRINCIPLE: Understand others by acknowledging their loss

When it's another person hurting, thinking about what they might have lost gives you patience and understanding of them. It helps you to better comprehend his or her actions. Again, that's not to excuse inappropriate or unkind behaviour, simply to explain it.

> "When people are the prickliest is when they need the most understanding."
> ~Marion Grobb Finkelstein

It's an explanation, not an excuse.

This understanding builds bridges between you and others. Instead of getting angry and disconnected from them, imagining the losses they're enduring will help you to maintain patience and possibly even preserve the relationship itself.

When you're able to overcome the emotions linked to your challenging situation or person, you'll be equipped to see the person or persons who offend you in a different light. You will actually have compassion for them as you view them from this new perspective. Assuming this unique vantage point, you'll see this difficult person as being stuck and in pain whereas you are freed. You've emancipated yourself by naming your losses and in doing so, are on your way to creating a new reality and mindset. You are learning coping skills the other person clearly doesn't have. They may never have. This is all the more reason why they need someone like you to appreciate their perspective.

When people are the prickliest is when they need the most understanding.

How to word it

You are now able to enunciate your loss and how it makes you feel. Now that you've got a grip on what's really bothering you, let's sum it up in one neat and tidy sentence. Here's the framework you can use as you fill in the blanks:

> "This is what happened / My situation is this (DESCRIBE in one or two sentences the nature of your challenge you're dealing with) _____. This situation makes me feel (INSERT your sentiment, e.g., angry, sad, upset, etc.) _____ because I feel like (INSERT some of your described losses) _____."

Let's look back at my personal example about not having children. In the course of normal introductions upon meeting new people, the topic often turns to children and if we have any. I typically respond by using the format above and simply say, "No, we don't have kids." In doing so, I'm describing the partial situation and I quite often leave it at that.

Sometimes I choose to elaborate and add an explanatory

comment. When I do, I use the format given above and say something such as, "It's not the way we planned it. It's just the card we got dealt", thereby fleshing out the challenge or disappointment. If I want to divulge more to a trusted confidante, I use the sentence structure I suggest above, share a personal piece of myself, and explain as follows:

> "Not having children will be my life's greatest regret. I miss the experience of being a mom. I feel like my life was rewritten without my permission. My greatest fear is being a vulnerable senior and having no one to advocate on my behalf. Although I have wonderful nieces and a nephew, they have their own lives and will be busy enough caring for their own children and aging parents. Therefore, I will place myself in care years before I actually need it because by the time I do, it will be too late. That saddens me and scares me a bit, but I know I'll figure it out".

Well, there you have it--my losses and fears normally shared with my closest of friends who care to ask. If delving that deeply into my life makes you feel uncomfortable, that's not my intent. I share these personal insights with you in the way of illustrating how profound defining your loss can be. Getting in touch with your fears and what you are mourning is your launchpad to move forward. Enunciating your fears and losses allows you to manage your expectations, prepare for the future, and decide where to spend your resources now to create the future that best serves you.

Use your situation and fill in the blanks with your own answers. Now you can understand your sense of loss and how to express it productively to those you wish to know.

Chapter 3 recap

- Your situation is robbing you from your goals;
- Life isn't controllable; your responses are;
- Admitting hurt is a strength;
- Acknowledging losses validates your pain;
- List your losses, fears, and ask, "then what?";
- Understand others by acknowledging their loss;
- Understanding a behaviour doesn't mean agreeing with it;
- Give voice to and validate your loss.

Now that you've defined your challenging situation and the losses you feel as a result of it, you're ready to move on to the next step--exploring your contributing role in creating or maintaining your difficult situation. It's a tough one, and I know you're up for it because you're tough too. You're resilient. You've already lived through countless difficult times many others wouldn't have handled so well. How do I know that? Because you're here right now.

CHAPTER 4

STEP 2, Q1: WHAT'S MY ROLE?

Replay, please (without guilt or regret)

What you're about to do is engage in the "four flipping questions" I've developed and affectionately call, the *Flip It Formula*™. These questions will help you flip just about any negative event into a positive outcome. Although these questions are simple, they aren't always easy--they may require great thought and effort on your part. Here's a sneak preview of the questions we'll be digging into in this and future chapters:

1. What is my role?
2. How could it be worse?
3. What's the gift?
4. What will I change in future?

This first question is what you're going to tackle here, in this chapter. As you work through the following chapters, you'll find that some of these questions may be easier than others for you to answer. Others will get you thinking in ways you've never considered before and will require you to stretch past your comfort zone and consider new perspectives. They may challenge your beliefs and most certainly will have an impact on your mindset and how you perceive and react to challenges. I invite you to come along for the journey. Participate. Throw up your arms and enjoy the ride. Each question is an opportunity for you to dive in and reflect on your tough situations and repeated patterns in your life ... and to change them. This is a chance for you to rip back the curtain and see aspects of yourself you may never have explored before.

In this question of defining your role, please remember this: Be kind to yourself.

I am cautious in sharing this step with you, concerned that you may pass harsh judgment on yourself. Please don't.

Flip It Formula™

STEP 1: Acknowledge the loss

STEP 2: Ask four flippin' questions
- 1) What is **my role**?
- 2) How could it be **worse**?
- 3) What's the **gift**?
- 4) What will I **change in future**?

That isn't the intent whatsoever. Rather, you are invited to consider these thoughts with an open, non-judgmental mind. It's all about stepping back and objectively looking at your actions, the impact they have on your goals and outcomes, and how you relate to others. Are you ready to do all that while ensuring that you're gentle with yourself? If so, terrific! Let's begin. If not, revisit the chapter on self-care and meet up with me here again when you're done.

What's your real-life example?

What was one of the most difficult times in your life? Think about an event or life circumstance that didn't turn out the way you had planned or expected. Perhaps it's a tough situation you're living at this very moment or maybe it's something from your distant past that still haunts you. It might be a workplace communication challenge such as a difficult boss, a client who's at loggerheads with you, or an employee with a bad attitude. Perhaps it's a personal life matter such as a difficult partner, an argumentative relative, or a noisy neighbour who is stealing the quiet enjoyment of your home. Maybe it's a missed goal of hitting that target weight, ending or starting a relationship, or moving to a new city. Whatever your situation, you didn't get what you'd hoped.

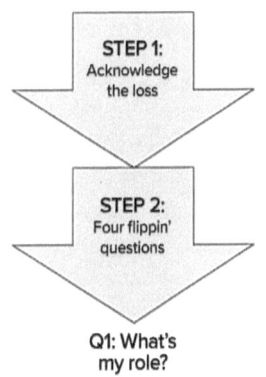

Think about a bullseye you want to hit and haven't (yet). You're putting lots of effort into achieving the outcome and the results you're getting are disappointing at best, discouraging at worst. You feel like a failure caught up in a terrible storm you can't seem to escape. You want to end the cycle and get relief and have tried everything you know. It's just not working. You're not getting the results you desire.

Hopefully, you've been following along and doing the exercises in this book. If writing out answers isn't your thing, I encourage you to still actively participate by giving them thought and applying them to your specific circumstances. That's what makes these approaches real and useful for you--using them.

Now that you have a specific difficult incident in mind, consider how you responded or are currently responding to it. During these times, you are playing a role. When a conflict arises or you're faced with a disappointment, your thoughts, actions, and words push you in a certain direction. How you behave helps to mold the outcome you experience. If you don't like the outcome, take a peek at your role.

Maybe you're contributing to your unwanted outcomes more than you realize.

How you contribute to your negative outcome

It's difficult to admit that you had an active part in the play that unfolded and led to the situation you're now living. "But wait, Marion," you exclaim. "It isn't my fault". And you might be right. Bad things befall good people. Someone treats you unfairly. Injuries happen. Economies crash. Circumstances you have no control over affect your life. All that is true.

However, how you *respond* to these uncontrollable factors plays a big part in creating your final result. Like it or not, you most certainly have a role. In fact, when it comes to your life, you're the star, the headliner, and the centre of your own universe. You have the leading role and the spotlight is on *you*. In fact, you play a part in every single outcome you experience.

It's not about pointing fingers: It's about taking responsibility and that is very different than assuming blame. You may have done what you did for very good reasons. You may have considered the other roads to take and chose this one as the least painful or the one you believed would ultimately lead to the greatest reward. When you assume responsibility and acknowledge your role, you take control.

Sometimes it's not what you say or do that contributes to a bad situation--it's what you don't. Those loving words you never shared with your partner create unwanted distance between you. Perhaps you refrain from reciprocating small gestures of kindness your employees extend to you and this serves to undermine teamwork and office morale. Maybe you're proud of your child's achievements yet never let him or her know. All these inactions contribute to your dissatisfying situation and define your role in helping to create or continue it.

The question about your role isn't about your intention: It's about actual behaviour. You may have intended to behave in an exact opposite manner and gotten carried away with the passion of the moment or succumbed to peer pressure. You may have said or not said, done or left undone, things you never thought you would. Consequently, the end result that you got was nowhere near what you had hoped it would be.

When you choose certain actions and responses, you choose the result. Your actions sets off a chain of responses from others which, in turn, create the outcomes you live. And so the dance began and continues.

Now, think specifically of one of your personal challenging situations. Put your emotions on hold for a moment and don your logical, objective cap. From that perspective, look at your situation and, without pointing fingers at yourself or others, pinpoint your beliefs and behaviours that may have snowballed the unsatisfactory result and the response you received.

Here's some circumstances you might relate to:

- You have a bully boss and you placidly take the abuse and remain silent;
- Your budget is cut and you don't present a business case against the cut explaining the value you offer for the budget you spend;
- You say you want to lose weight, yet sneak in your treats when no one's looking;
- You accuse your spouse of being distant while you constantly point out what you see as his or her faults.

Yes, you have reasons for behaving the way you do, whether it is taking action that doesn't work, or taking no action at all. You are stressed. You do what seems reasonable at the time. Perhaps your choices are based on the path of least resistance. Maybe they are fed by pent-up emotion that finally erupts and demands to be heard. Whatever your situation and how you handle it, don't judge yourself; just 'fess up to your role, not whether it was right or wrong. Simply report it.

EXAMPLE: Driving with my spouse (a.k.a., driving him crazy)

It would be a pretty safe statement to say that I generously give, shall we say, "driving suggestions" to my other half. My husband Steve doesn't need a GPS--he's got me and I am ever ready to offer a running commentary on traffic conditions and directions. (Anyone relate?)

The other day we are driving down a four-lane road and, to me, it feels like Steve all of a sudden brakes in the middle of the lane. Admittedly, it isn't a jolting or violent stop, just a puzzling one. My response? I look up from checking my email on my mobile and exclaim excitedly, "What's happening? What are you doing?" I can't figure out why he has come to a dead stop with traffic whizzing by in the neighboring lanes. I think for sure there must be something wrong. Steve looks at me incredulously and says with a touch of impatience and disbelief, "Nothing's wrong. I'm turning". Without a signal?, I think silently. Stopping without explanation? What?! I feel like his silence is totally disregarding my presence or the impact of his actions on me. Meanwhile, he's likely thinking I'm a nervous wreck and making him nervous in the process.

After a moment, I realize that my concern is over the top. Well, in honesty, it is a few hours later that I have this admission realization. Once the emotion has passed and I am able to look rationally at what had happened, I can see that I had contributed to the less than ideal outcome by overreacting to a very simple stop. Yes, it would have been appreciated if he'd said something and explained. Yes, I would have liked his acknowledging my perspective. Even an apology for a sudden stop would have been welcomed. I could continue rattling on about things he could have done but that's not what I want to do as I remind myself to begin by looking at my own actions, not his. With this in mind, I admit to myself and later to Steve that my reaction isn't in measure with his action (or inaction of saying nothing).

Remember, the focus of this exercise isn't to point fingers at myself or someone else: It's to focus on my role without judgement and with full responsibility. Doing this, I can see from an objective perspective that it would look and feel like I had overreacted and contributed to escalating the tensions. I define and accept my role. That doesn't mean I like it or am proud of it. It means that I claim and own my actions.

Epilogue: Don't worry about the outcome of this situation. Once I accepted my role and explained my reaction to Steve, he understands. My role that fed this negative outcome was born of several fender benders from years before. Since then, I admit that I'm a nervous passenger. That's my homework. That's my responsibility to fix that piece and remove or tame that trigger. I acknowledge how this part of my past is affecting my present and it's up to me to manage it. Looking at my role helps me discover this insight.

Let me be clear here--Steve didn't like my reaction (and frankly, neither did I). However, because I'm now able to enunciate my role and take responsibility for it, he now understands where my reaction comes from. Using this approach of acknowledging my role opens up conversation between us and we each learn.

On the upside, I'm pretty sure Steve has since forgotten all about his threat to never drive me anywhere again. Ever.

So what is *your* role in your situation? What pieces of your past are triggers that you want to wrestle to the ground? Value those sides of you because they are clues as to why you behave the way you do. Those clues will unlock the doors that will lead you to different and better outcomes. You behave the way you do for a reason. Figure out what that reason is and you'll have the key to change that behaviour. Even if you never know the exact reason why your ineffective reaction comes to the forefront, at least you know the behaviour to change.

EXAMPLE: Boss keeps you waiting

Suppose you have a boss who routinely keeps you waiting outside his or her office for meetings. You sit there, anxious about all the items on your desk requiring attention and the opportunity cost of you twiddling your thumbs as your boss carries on chatting on the phone with another colleague. This seems to be your boss's modus operandi. It's just the way he rolls.

Once you've defined your difficult situation, now you ask, "What's my role?" At first blush, you may think nothing at all. It's the boss who's not behaving properly, not you. Think again. Keep in mind the purpose of this question isn't to assign blame to you or any other parties. Instead, ask yourself what are you doing that's contributing to this frustrating situation? Assuming this perspective helps you to grab back some control.

Perhaps you answer that your role in creating this outcome is that you are spending your energy getting ticked off, insulted, and feeling discounted. Your blood pressure is rising and your anxiety is through the roof.

Maybe you've contributed unknowingly to this situation by tolerating it without saying anything. Perhaps your role in creating or perpetuating this situation and outcome may be not what you did but rather what you didn't do. You never mention to your boss the impact of his actions on your effectiveness. You have a role.

EXAMPLE: Medical challenge

Your challenge may be a physical one. You may be experiencing an illness or medical condition of some sort. What could your role possibly be in that? Without passing judgment or sentencing yourself to the harsh burden of guilt, objectively step back and ask what you did or didn't do that may have been a step toward the outcome. What you're looking at is a missed goal. In this case, the goal is having good health.

Your role could have been in missing the warning signs. Maybe you didn't listen to your body when it was whispering before it had to scream to get your attention. Perhaps you hadn't learned from a similar previous experience you or someone close to you had lived. Maybe it was a question of lifestyle choices you made that could have been different resulting in a different outcome. Maybe you mistakenly thought self-care was selfish (it's not) and didn't put yourself and your own health on the agenda as you were so busy taking care of everyone else.

It's important to identify whatever small thing you might have done, or something that you didn't do, that contributed to your goal being missed and to creating your negative outcome. Why? Because, when you take responsibility for your piece, you take control of the wheel and can begin turning your ship around.

If you believe that your results are everyone else's fault, you have no reason to change. Assume responsibility for your role and you regain control of your life and your outcomes.

WHAT'S MY ROLE?

This next example is one that Steve and I lived a number of years ago. It demonstrates how things go awry and is quintessential *Finkelstein Factor*™ material. In other words, things we never could have anticipated came to pass and threw us for a loop. Even though your situation is quite different, note how this story takes unexpected and unpleasant twists and turns, just as your life goes in unwanted directions from time to time. After you read it, we'll talk about what your role is and how you can apply these principles to you and your life.

EXAMPLE: Shadow Finkelstein gets snipped

Steve and I are animal lovers. We both grew up with dogs and cats throughout most of our lives. As a young couple, we decide to adopt an adult cat, about about a year old. We reason that kittens are adopted quickly whereas the older cats are last to be chosen and need the homes the most. When we visit the shelter and his little black paw comes up to touch our hands on the cage, we know that this cat is meant to be ours. We name him Shadow.

Even though we intend to keep Shadow indoors, we decide to get him neutered just in case he somehow gets loose. A couple weeks later, on the designated morning, we wake up early before work, put Shadow into his cage, and drop him off at the veterinarian's to undergo the procedure.

Several hours pass and I receive a phone call from the vet's receptionist with some bad news: The doctor is in the middle of the operation and discovers that Shadow's left testicle hasn't dropped. Say what? She continues. He needs more surgery at an additional cost. Do I approve? I reluctantly give permission and she advises that Shadow will be fine and to pick him up at the pre-set time later that afternoon. Perfect.

Steve and I arrive at the animal hospital a few minutes early to take care of the paperwork and payments before we collect our furry patient. When we approach the receptionist and identify ourselves, she shakes and lowers her head, casting her eyes downward in a concerned fashion. She makes timid eye contact and in a somber voice explains that, in addition to the testicular troubles, they find that Shadow is infested with fleas. Oh my. This requires not only a special kit to bathe him thoroughly, but a house kit to rid our residence of these biting bugs.

Oh nooooo! I feel my head spinning with the spectre of no sleep. If you've ever bathed a cat, you know what a delightful task that is (not)--and Shadow still had his claws. I envisioned us doing laundry until the wee morning hours, grabbing two hours of sleep, then showering and going in to the office. I saw us sprinkling flea powder into every crevice in our place, hoping this would rid our home and Shadow of the fleas.

Just as I am absorbing the requirement of our impending chores, the receptionist tells us how much these additional services and products tally--a staggering amount for such a tiny little guy. We swallow hard and Steve pulls out his credit card. I'm pretty sure I saw him tremble as he handed it over.

Once all payment is done, the receptionist rises to get Shadow as we head to the waiting room in anticipation of his grand arrival. Moments later, she reappears holding an exhausted looking cat, with no two hairs pointing in the same direction. Steve and I take a look and bellow in unison, "That's not Shadow!"

Stunned, the receptionist runs to her desk holding the mangy critter and with an incredulous expression, sputters that they've had several Shadows checked in that very day for the same procedure. That may well be, but the last name of this Shadow she's holding isn't Finkelstein.

WHAT'S MY ROLE?

The receptionist disappears into the back rooms and emerges with a beautiful, long-haired, black, beautifully groomed, and gratefully flea-free feline. Shadow is a little worse for the wear from the day, and likely not too happy with how his day is going, but ours just got tremendously better.

As we pull away from the vet's office, I find myself wondering if the other owners like the testicular procedure I approved.

What was our role in this mess? It may take some time for you to have the perspective to step back and answer this question. The more you practice this skill, the easier and quicker the answers will come to you. From this vantage point of distance and objectivity, you could define our role in this event as being any of the following:

- We named our cat a very common name, unknowingly feeding into the chance for mix-ups;
- When the receptionist calls to ask about the procedure, it never occurs to me to verify Shadow by description or last name, though I could have easily done that;
- Before we paid for anything, I could have asked to see Shadow.

Note how there is no guilt or finger-pointing. Just facts. I use the word, "unknowingly" when describing our roles. The same is true in your challenge. You may not realize the ripple effect of your actions. You may not understand how far-reaching the good or bad impact will or could be on yourself and others. You may have zero intent to feed into a bad outcome, yet you may do so without knowing it. This fact allows you to review your situation and your role objectively and most importantly, without guilt or regret.

An explanation isn't an excuse

There's a difference between an explanation and an excuse. Defining your default response and your role in a situation is an explanation and allows you to assume responsibility. The finesse comes in doing this without guilt or regret. You can't change or rewrite the past but you can certainly change what isn't working for you in the future. As painful as it may be, defining your role in creating a bad outcome frees you to explore alternate strategies for the future.

When you're going through this exercise of defining your role, it's critical to understand that explaining your role doesn't excuse your or someone else's behaviour. Just because you may not have spoken up, it doesn't justify someone else belittling you. You may have unknowingly played into facilitating the other person's or your own dysfunctional behaviour. Again, this doesn't excuse your or the other person's behaviour, it simply helps to explain it. It's an explanation, not an excuse.

Keep the memory, leave the emotion

Emotion equals motion. It gives energy and is a force to be reckoned with. Like any source of power, one is well advised to treat emotion with respect and to channel it in productive ways. Just as electricity is powerful and can transform lives, so too can emotion. Electricity can also harm if not harnessed correctly, and that is also true of emotion.

Your life's most challenging moments are inextricably linked with strong emotion. The very nature of difficult times necessitates you drawing on emotional reserve to pull through them. That's why you feel exhausted during or sometimes after a trying episode. This emotion can anchor you to negative feelings and behaviours associated with that particular trigger or action from someone else. Whenever that emotional button gets pushed, you revert to the behaviour you know, even though your rational self admits that this behaviour isn't getting you the results you want. It may not make pragmatic sense, but at that point you're operating from an emotional plane, not a logical one.

The key? Remove the emotion. Disconnect those links between your event, your emotions, and typical default response. You may now create new associations and responses that will better serve your desired outcome. You can anchor your emotion to positive outcomes and behaviours instead.

Neuroscientist, Dr. Joe Dispanza, is a teacher and author of several New York Times best-sellers. He helps people understand how their beliefs, perceptions and energy fields affect their outcomes and relationships with others. In one of his many YouTube videos, he states, "The memory without the emotional charge is wisdom."[3]

Being mired in emotion is holding you chained to the past, stopping you from moving forward. Look at the dynamics of whatever your situation is, whatever happened, and do so without the emotion and most certainly, without any judgement. From this perspective, ask:

- Why might the other person have behaved as she or he did?
- Why do you react the way you do?
- Why doesn't your response work?

---

[3] You can watch this video at https://youtu.be/0AsGxWFD7pk

Examine without emotion both your role and that of others. People behave the way they do for a reason, and that includes you. (Remember, that's an explanation, not an excuse for inappropriate actions).

It was in the previous step of defining your loss that you confronted your emotions. You faced them head on and put words around them to describe and name them. Now is the time to put that emotion aside, and look at your situation again, this time, from an objective, non-emotional perspective. It takes a conscious effort and gets easier with the passage of time from that emotional event. At the time you're living through a difficult situation, this is exceptionally difficult to do, though I encourage you to give it a go.

Keep the memory, define the emotion attached to it, and then let the emotion go. When you rid yourself of that emotional charge associated with your event and hurt, you leave with the lesson and surrender the pain. You move forward wiser and one big step closer to where you deserve to be.

Acknowledge and then forgive

Acknowledging your role is only half of the equation. The other half is forgiving yourself. You did or are doing the best you can at a given time, with the knowledge, resources, and skills you currently have or had at that moment.

We will talk a great deal more about forgiveness later with actual steps to take you there. For now, suffice to say that you deserve the gift of forgiveness for whatever actions or inactions you committed. Being kind to yourself is part of self-care and you deserve that.

Chapter 4 recap

- What are you doing or not doing that contributes to your negative outcome?
- An explanation isn't an excuse
- Keep the memory, leave the emotion
- Acknowledge and then forgive

Coming up next, we'll be talking about how to flip your attitude to one of appreciation, even when things appear dire. You're going to continue looking at your past and present situation as I guide you through the steps to move into the future. You'll learn how to get the most out of your biggest challenge and your everyday frustrations. Don't worry: There's a light at the end of the tunnel and, for once, it's not a train. Time to walk toward it and come out the other side.

CHAPTER 5

STEP 2, Q2: HOW COULD IT BE WORSE?
Develop an attitude of gratitude

Life doesn't always go in the direction you plan and this diversion can result in anything from a minor disappointment to a major life alteration. You do the best you can with what you know and the skills you possess at the time. Accepting this premise, logic would then argue if what you're doing isn't working and getting the results you want, gaining more knowledge and learning different skills will increase your chances of doing so. Hence the reason you're reading this book, right?

> "When life humbles you to your knees is when you plant yourself and grow."
> ~Marion Grobb Finkelstein

You may be in a place right now where, in spite of all your efforts, you find yourself sinking deeper into a black hole. You can't seem to find your way out. Sound familiar? It should. We all have moments like that. Find solace in knowing you're not alone. If you can't stand your situation, whatever it might be, that's fantastic because this discontentment is the mojo that will act as your motivation to change.

Knowing you have those tools in your life kit will brace you for the storm and give you confidence in facing it. Changing your mindset will help you manage. If you're not living a tough time right now, bravo to you for preparing yourself for whatever may be coming down the road.

Often in our youth, we think nothing bad will touch us. We look at others facing difficult times and sigh with compassion, silently thanking our lucky stars that we're not that unfortunate. If you relate to that thinking, know that the techniques, strategies, and perspectives I share will not only help you build compassion for others, they will also prepare you for your own personal struggles should your circumstances change. In a sense, consider what you're learning now as insurance against the unexpected.

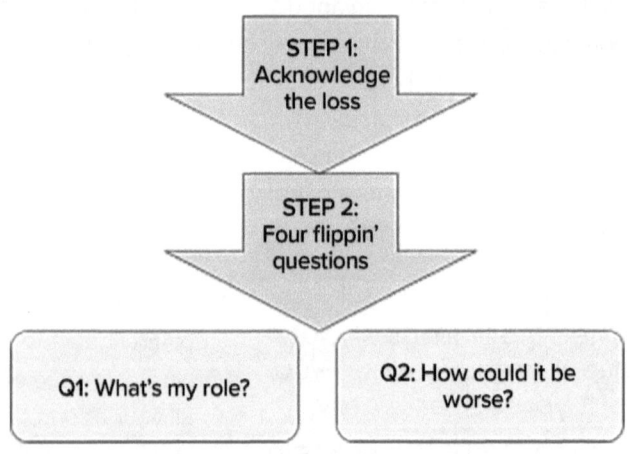

When things go wrong, it's not all bad news. Remember this: When life humbles you to your knees is the very moment to plant yourself and grow. And yes, at times life hurts--that's why it's called *growing pains*. Growth is often accompanied with discomfort. Stepping out of that comfort zone requires stretching and using muscles you may not have exercised in a long time, if at all. Give it a go. You got this.

Before we get to the next exercise, let's recap what we've covered so far. You now know that self-care is healthy and necessary. You have defined your life challenge and acknowledge the loss and deep hurt you feel at its hands. You take responsibility for your role in contributing to this situation and you do so without guilt or judgment.

> 'Becoming aware of all the ways a situation could be worse prepares a rich soil to plant the seeds of gratitude."
> ~Marion Grobb Finkelstein

And now, another tough question: How could it be worse? I asked this question to a friend of mine and she was a little taken aback by it. She had just confided in me about the heartbreak of her relationship with her husband. When I posed the question, she shot back with a question of her own asking, *how on earth could this question be helpful?* I asked her to humour me and play along which she begrudgingly did. As she began to name all the ways her situation could be worse, she got it: By surrendering to this process she was preparing a rich soil to plant the seeds of gratitude. Consciously acknowledging how much worse things could be makes you thankful that it's not.

Here's an example that will help you walk through your own situation from a perspective of gratitude. It fleshes out my friend's story. To preserve her privacy, like all the stories I share in this book, with the exception of my own, names and a few details have been changed. The lesson remains the same.

Debbie's divorce

Debbie is a big believer in the law of attraction. She uses everything she has read on the topic and learns to manifest in her life the man she thought would be the perfect lifemate. For nine years he truly is. They enjoy the arts community, are active in local social circles, and co-own several thriving businesses. Their lives are intertwined and beautifully compatible on every level ... until they slowly begin to grow apart. He is spending more time with his friends and Debbie is left puzzled and feeling alone. He isn't as physically demonstrative as he had once been and she feels like she is living in an emotional desert.

How could it be worse?

After some reflection, Debbie acknowledges that the bad situation could have gone on for longer. He could be having an affair, or several of them, over the years. Or if he, in fact, is unfaithful, he could be flagrantly flaunting it, adding further to Debbie's sense that she will surely be the talk of the town and has been played for a fool. It could have been worse if she had not had the opportunity to enjoy nine years of happiness prior to this. Her situation would be more dire if she were left destitute like many women after a split-up. She could be completely alone without the support of friends and family.

As you read this story, you may be thinking, *how on earth could this exercise be helpful to me?* Let me reassure you that taking time to write out your list of how things could be worse, or at minimum, to give it great thought, will release your stress. It will allow you to face your fears and grapple them to the ground. Take a moment now and view your particular challenge through the lens of *how could it be worse?* How would *you* respond?

Just think about that for a moment or two. Wrap your head around it and let it rattle around in your mind. When taken from that perspective, how would you answer and what would you include on your list of worse outcomes? Live it, allow the emotions to run through you. Let your mind wander to the most devastating situation you truly fear. Don't worry--you're not going to live there for long. The future steps in the *Finkelstein Factor*^{TM} process and *Flip It Formula*^{TM} will pull you from this depressing place. Consider it a necessary stepping stone to hop across troubled waters and bring you to the other side.

Let's look at another example, this time, a work-based one.

Flirtatious Frank

Peggy works in a busy national office as a mid-level manager. She's well respected by her clients and colleagues, except for one. Her peer, Frank, never seems to miss an opportunity to give her up-and-down stares and inappropriate sexual comments. Peggy has spoken to him privately to no avail. He's scoffed off her concerns as being overly sensitive to his so-called jokes. In spite of her explaining that his unwanted attention is inappropriate and unprofessional, his behaviour continues. She is angry and feels disrespected and shares this sentiment with her other colleagues and boss who in turn, speaks to Frank's boss insisting that this behaviour doesn't reflect well on Frank or the organization. Her boss argues that these actions are inconsistent with the company's values.

How could it be worse?

In this situation, Peggy may not have been supported by her supervisor. He may have scoffed it off as not a big deal without seriously considering her perspective. Frank's actions and remarks could be more frequent, louder, and with an audience.

Heaven forbid, he could have acted this way in shared meetings with clients. It could have escalated further to physical abuse. These actions may have tarnished the organization's impeccable reputation. Peggy may not have had the support of colleagues and confidantes to help guide her. She may not have had the maturity and life experience to handle the situation as competently as she does.

As bad as it is, it could definitely be worse.

In this story and the one prior to it, we look at how things could be worse in a personal life situation and then, in a work-related one. These principles and exercises I'm sharing with you are equally effective in either environment, and likewise, with life's small irritants as well as major life challenges.

As you walk through these stories with me, of course you won't relate to every detail because your story is unique. However, I do encourage you to take away the lesson of how to apply these steps to your own life.

Now, let's have a little fun. This next example is light-hearted and snitched from my husband's experiences. It's not a life-altering event, just a small incident that demonstrates how this thinking of *how could it be worse* helps you cope and kicks in almost immediately, once you get used to adopting this mindset.

Steve's bus bust

When our nephew is in his early twenties, Steve decides to surprise Josh with a weeklong golf holiday down south. Oh, how they look forward to some quality uncle-nephew time as well as escaping the harsh cold of Canadian winters.

Shortly after they check into the resort, Steve goes to the front desk and asks how to catch the courtesy shuttle bus to the nearby golf course. The friendly clerk explains that all he needs to do is reserve a time and go sit on the bench to wait. That certainly sounds easy enough, Steve thinks, so he requests a pick-up later that day. In plenty of time, Josh and Steve go to their room, grab their clubs, and proceed to wait on the designated bench. And wait. And wait. Long after the scheduled pickup hour and afraid they would miss their tee-off time, they decide to walk instead, carrying their clubs all the way.

After the game, Steve asks the pro shop at the golf course how to get back to the resort. The staff member explains that they have a telephone to request the courtesy shuttle that is included for all their guests. Steve picks up the phone and hears, "Si" on the other end. He requests the shuttle back to the hotel and the voice on the phone explains that the shuttle will be there in fifteen minutes. They wait for twenty, then walk.

This story repeats itself for seven days straight. They never catch the shuttle. Out of the fourteen possible lifts, they get none.

Instead of bemoaning their misfortune, Steve chooses to acknowledge the fact that it could always be worse with comments such as, "Well, at least we're not waiting for a bus in winter weather", "Thank goodness we're close enough to walk to the golf course", and, "It's a good thing we don't have a lot of heavy clubs in our bags."

The additional good thing this unlucky incident brings, is a funny story he tells others in future years.

It's at this point in the story, that is, when disturbing events occur multiple times, that many people would be angry, ticked off, and want some sort of compensation. Some people would react by simply throwing up their arms in frustration and simply giving up. What would your reaction be?

Instead of assuming a negative spiral, Steve chooses to see the humour immediately and guffaws at the situation. It becomes the daily joke between uncle and nephew, forever branding the memory of this trip with humour and appreciation. He and our nephew never find out why the shuttle goes astray which only adds to the hilarity of the story as they recount it to great peels of laughter at many family get-togethers.

Steve and Josh come back with many stories. In fact, it was these very tales that prompted me to coin the phrase, *the Finkelstein Factor*™, because so many things went wrong and they figured them out with grace and laughter. Steve benefited from the finely tuned skill of flipping negatives into positive and creating funny anecdotes. He innately understood that things could be worse. The situations that would set many people into a downward spin were fodder for giggles.

What about you and your challenges? Are you able to see how things could be worse and that, just maybe, they're not quite as bad as you had first imagined? Give it a try. This thinking may not come naturally at first, though I assure you, with practice it will be second nature. Use it with a challenge you're currently facing. If you don't have a situation that pops immediate to mind, you will think of something later. It could be a major something, or perhaps a small irritant. It might be someone who keeps you waiting longer than you expected. Or a client who doesn't respond. Perhaps it's a missed opportunity of some sort.

How could it be worse? Think about it. Brainstorm with a friend. Write it down. Whatever approach works best for you.

So, what's the "DIF"?

When you're developing your own list based on your particulars, think about how your situation could be worse in terms of duration, intensity, and frequency. To remember these dimensions, use the acronym "DIF", as in "what DIF does it make?", with the letters representing "D" for "duration", "I" for "intensity", and "F" for "frequency".

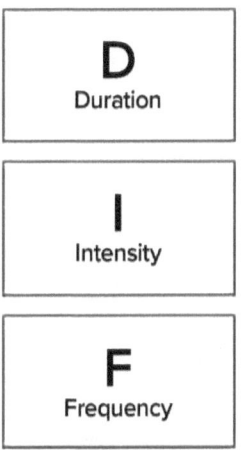

These parameters will help you to dig in and amplify your situation, permitting you to easily develop your own list of how things could be worse. The duration could be longer of something unpleasant or shorter of something you enjoyed. The intensity of your hurt or the degree of damage you experienced could have been or could be much deeper and severe. The frequency of this type of negative event could be much higher or, conversely, a pleasant situation could have occurred much less frequently, if at all.

If you enjoy unpacking details and assuming a pragmatic approach, you may find it easier to enunciate how your circumstance could be worse by examining your situation in terms of:

- Bad aspects (that could have been longer, more intense, more frequent)
- Good aspects (that could have been a shorter duration, less intense, less frequent)

When you look at Debbie's case mentioned previously, you're able to cluster her list of "worse" items into these two groups as follows:

- Bad aspects (that could have been worse by being longer, more intense, more frequent)
    - The distance between them could have gone on for longer than it did (duration)
    - He could have had an affair, or if several of them, over the years (intensity, frequency)
    - If he was having an affair, he could have flagrantly flaunted it (intensity)
    - She could have been left destitute like many women after a split-up (intensity)

- Good aspects (that could have been worse by being a shorter duration, less intense, less frequent)
    - The nine years of wonderful memories could have been more short-lived (duration)
    - She could be completely alone without the support of friends and family (Intensity)
    - They could have gone on fewer trips and social events than they enjoyed (frequency)

Everyone thinks differently. If you find the above approach too structured, don't use it. If you prefer freestyling your list and writing down a conscious stream of brainstormed ideas of how your situation could be worse, terrific. This creative approach will work if you enjoy a process without a lot of structure and formality.

On the other hand, if it helps you organize your thoughts and you prefer a more systematic approach to develop your list, I encourage you to create a chart like the one below to get your ideas flowing.

Q2: How could it be worse?	GOOD ASPECTS (that could be worse by being shorter, less intense, and less frequent)	BAD ASPECTS (that could be worse by being longer, more intense, and more frequent)
Duration		
Intensity		
Frequency		

You may find using a chart too formal for your taste, or perhaps even complicated to your way of thinking. We're all blessedly different and receive and process information in our own unique ways. Use whatever approach speaks to you.

If you're grappling with a difficult situation right now, take a few moments and a crack at developing your list of how things could be worse. These *Flip It Formula*™ steps and the *Finkelstein Factor*™ process become more real and certainly more useful when you begin to apply them to your own life. I have.

Here's an example of how I used this 'how could it be worse" step in the process. It involves a very difficult and painful medical condition I experienced a few years ago.

Marion's disc disaster

During a conference in Halifax, Nova Scotia, it hits. I am delivering several plenary sessions to a hundred or more project managers.

HOW COULD IT BE WORSE?

I haven't slept much at all the night before and I'm not too concerned as I figure it is just the travel catching up with me. No biggie. I deliver my keynote in the morning and then at noon go to my room hoping to catch a power nap before my afternoon presentation. It is no use. Every time I put my head to pillow or rest horizontally, the cervical discs press against my nerves and the pain is beyond excruciating, It radiates from my neck down my shoulders and both arms. It discover a newfound understanding for that expression, "getting on my nerves"! Something is horribly wrong. I manage to get through my afternoon presentations and then dread the return flight and having to contend with lifting my carry-on luggage into the overhead bins. I call my doctor before I even leave the hotel to return home. The flight is torturesome.

When I arrive back in Ottawa, I can't sleep at all. Thankfully, I see my doctor the very next day. She prescribes medication that does nothing. The doctor, chiropractor, physiotherapist, acupuncturist, and massage therapist offer little, if any, relief. I resign myself to chronic pain and pray it ends.

It takes about four months for the pain to resolve itself, during which time I continue to work. In addition, we are in the midst of moving from a three-bedroom home we'd lived in for seventeen years (this means lots of accumulated items!). We have a household to be packed and I have no idea how I am ever going to manage.

I get through this episode and then, about a year later, it repeats itself for another four months, again resolving itself and dodging the recommended neurological surgery to fuse together the discs.

When I was living through this, I was afraid it would last forever. The pain was so intense, I wasn't sure how much longer I could take it. My greatest fear was that it would continue, that this was my new normal or, heaven bid, that it would get worse. The thought was unimaginable. I now understood chronic pain and the desperation it brings. It morphs your personality, zaps your energy, and robs you of joy.

It was almost impossible for me to maintain hope. Almost. Then I started thinking about how much worse it could be and generated a rather extensive list. Here's a sample of that collection of thoughts to give you an idea of how this question works. For purposes of demonstration, I have sorted them into the suggested chart, but remember, you don't need to use this chart if you don't want to.

Q2: How could it be worse?	GOOD ASPECTS (that could be worse by being shorter, less intense, and less frequent). It could be worse if ... (the good aspects didn't exist)	BAD ASPECTS (that could be worse by being longer, more intense, and more frequent) It could be worse if ... (the bad aspect was longer, more intense, more frequent)
Duration	It could be worse if ... I had never had years of great health before these episodes	It could be worse if ... it lasted more than 4 months... the chronic pain and health issues could have started earlier in my life and lasted longer
Intensity	It could be worse if ... I had to pack my moving boxes all by myself, or if I had more boxes to pack	It could be worse if ... it were more painful, more severe, more debilitating. It could have affected more parts of my body, traveled down my spine, affecting the sciatic nerve and both legs
Frequency	It could be worse if ... my health team professionals weren't available to treat me as often as required, or if I didn't have medical coverage	It could be worse if ... I had experienced many more occurences than just two in my lifetime

Writing your list is the key to moving yourself into a powerful mindset. It reminds you that no matter your situation or how bad it is, no matter how much you're going through at this time, that you have the strength and choice to get through this. It shifts your thinking from that of being victimized and "oh poor me" to "hey, I can do this". Yes, you can.

Please don't think for a moment that this step in any way is meant to make light of your difficulties or trivialize what you're living. It's difficult. Of course, it is. The purpose of this "how could it be worse" step is simply to flip your mindset to focus on what you do control--your attitude. Remember, the very first step of this whole *Flip It Formula*™ and *Finkelstein Factor*™ process is to acknowledge your loss, to get in touch with and recognize your pain.

This chapter is all about flipping your pain into power.

> "This step in no way is intended to trivialize your situation".
> ~Marion Grobb Finkelstein

I hope that you are able to apply everything you're learning to a particular struggle you're confronting right now. When you're exploring how your situation could be worse, I've offered you a couple approaches to use. Pick the one that speaks most to you. Go freestyle and purge your thoughts into a free-form list if that's your style, or use more structured and systematic approach with the chart I've offered. Whatever speaks to you. How you get there really doesn't matter. Answering the question, "how could it be worse?" does.

How to word it

How things could be worse is really a question to be answered by you, for you. It's not intended to be for the benefit of others. This question helps to shift your mindset and gets you ready to take the next few steps. The answers you've written for your "worse" list are a step in the whole process. This list is for your eyes and affects how you communicate with yourself. You may choose to share it with others and incorporate "It could be worse" statements into your language if you would find that useful and only if you would find that useful.

Just remember, before you productively express yourself with others, you must be able to speak constructively to yourself. Your self-talk sets the foundation for you to build healthy relationships and communication with others.

The benefit of using, "at least"

The two small words, "at least", will change your life. They will reframe how you look at difficult situations and change your mindset to one of gratitude and positivity. When you preface a sentence with "at least", you are shifting from a victim mindset to that of a victor. With that short phrase, you acknowledge that it could be worse and that there is some good to be found in your situation after all. You are telling your mind and body to breathe a sigh of relief.

CAUTION: Using the "at least" sentence is only to be done after your pain and loss is duly noted and acknowledged, per the first step. I can't emphasize this strongly enough. If you skip over this preliminary step, you will be trivializing your pain. If you push it into the background like this, you're not dealing with it. Please, ensure that you move to this "at least" statement only after you've worked through that first critical step of putting words to your loss.

HOW COULD IT BE WORSE?

Once you're ready, now you can assemble your exercises and use them to express yourself in a simple and succinct sentence. Using what you've defined as the good and bad aspects of your situation, you simply add the words "at least" before them and structure the sentence to express gratitude.

Using a very systematic approach, let's look at the chart we created in the previous chapter, building onto it and adding the "gifts", and using the term, "at least".

Q2: How could it be worse?	GOOD ASPECTS It could be worse if ... (the good aspects were shorter, less intense, less frequent)	AT LEAST ...	BAD ASPECTS It could be worse if ... (the bad aspects were longer, more intense, more frequent)	AT LEAST ...
Duration	It could be worse if ... I had never had years of great health before these episodes	At least ... I'd enjoyed years of good health before this.	It could be worse if ... it lasted more than 4 months... the chronic pain and health issues could have started earlier in my life and lasted longer	At least ... Each episode only lasted four months and is was during the summer, a slow time in my business.
Intensity	It could be worse if ... I had to pack my moving boxes all by myself, or if I had more boxes to pack	At least ... Friends helped me pack and I didn't have too many boxes as I'd purged a lot of items.	It could be worse if ... it were more painful, more severe, more debilitating. It could have affected more parts of my body, traveled down my spine, affecting the sciatic nerve and both legs	At least ... I was able to move my arms a bit and it didn't also travel down to both legs.

Frequency	It could be worse if ... my health team	At least ... My medical pros were readily available and provided through my government or covered by my medical plan.	It could be worse if ... I had experienced many more occurences than just two in my lifetime	At least ... It occurred only two times in my life and I've had years of relief since the last episode.

Putting it into a sentence

Using your chart as a source, or simply freestyling it, you can phrase your *how could it be worse* statement as follows:

"(STATE the situation then follow up with ...) At least (OR luckily/ well/ thank goodness/ I'm grateful that ...I) it/ we/ they *aren't* _____ (fill in what a WORST CASE would be)

... OR And, at least/well/luckily/thank heavens/I'm grateful it/we/ they *are* _____ (fill in the GOOD ASPECTS of what you do have and are grateful for)".

Given the above case studies, here's how they could be worded:

"I'm getting a divorce because my husband and I grew apart. At least he was amenable to a respectful breakup and I have a supportive family and network to help me through this".

"My boss is a jerk who repeatedly makes inappropriate and unwanted advances toward me. I'm grateful he's the only one like that in our organization and I have a supportive Human Resources colleague who is helping me through it".

> "We missed the shuttle bus for seven days straight. Luckily, it was great weather and our clubs weren't too heavy to carry and we were close enough to walk to the golf course".

> "I had two summers of cervical spine issues and debilitating radiopathy down both arms. Thank goodness it only lasted only four months each time and never returned. Even though I was in the middle of moving, thank goodness I had friends to help me pack".

Now, time for you to try it with whatever challenge you're handling. Describe the situation and follow it with an "at least" statement, flipping your negative into recognizing that it could always be worse.

Soon as you preface a sentence with "at least", an expression of appreciation is going to follow. Acknowledging how things could be worse makes you consciously aware not of what you don't have, but rather, what you do. It shifts you from a state of hopelessness to one where you are better able to cope and manage. It fosters an attitude of gratitude.

Chapter 5 recap

- Being aware of how a situation could be worse fosters an attitude of gratitude
- Define how things could be worse by examining your situation in terms of:
    - Bad aspects (that could have been longer, more intense, more frequent)
    - Good aspects (that could have been a shorter, less intense, less frequent)
- Brainstorm freestyle or use a structured chart ... use whatever process works for you

- When you preface a sentence with "at least", a statement of appreciation is going to follow
- Be sure not to jump to this "at least" exercise until you work through the step of acknowledging your loss so as not to trivialize your situation.

In the next chapter, you'll discover yet another way to use your "worse" list to move you forward. There's something wonderful waiting for you. Curious? Let's go there now.

CHAPTER 6

STEP 2, Q3: WHAT'S THE GIFT?
Reaping the reward

When life bears down upon you without reason, without rhyme, you may think it's impossible for something good to come from that experience. And you would be wrong. Just because you can't see the good at a certain moment doesn't mean it doesn't exist. There is a gift in your situation waiting for you. All you need to do is grab it and unwrap it.

The more difficult the situation, the more difficult it may be to see your gift. Find solace in knowing that although this may be true, it's also true that the bigger the challenge, the bigger the gift.

> "The bigger the challenge, the bigger the gift".
> ~Marion Grobb Finkelstein

Think about the last time you were mired in a very painful circumstance or what you may be living through right now. You could be ending a relationship. Maybe it is a nasty client who is stopping you from finalizing a very lucrative contract with your company. Or perhaps it's a personal health goal that you struggle to attain and are missing.

When you are living in an emotionally-charged situation, it is tough to shift your attention from your heart to your brain. This is the reason, in part, that I have written this book in a very systematic and logical fashion. It nudges you to stimulate the logical part of your brain, the part that will offer perspective when your heart is breaking and crying to you. It prepares you to follow a step-by-step system and engage in logical thinking that best serves you in decision-making. Tapping into your logical brain balances out the call of your heart.

Taking a small step away from the emotional tempest you're living allows you to look at your situation from a more objective viewpoint. It permits you to benefit from your logical self and to assume a different and more neutral vantage point. This, in turn, provides you with a different perspective and the ability to see things that you had previously overlooked. It's from this position that you are better placed to see your gift.

What exactly is "a gift"?

The gift in your situation is all about acknowledging not only how it could be worse but moving beyond to focus on what you have learned. What's the lesson you can take as you charge forward? The gift is in getting the message out of the mess. If you don't, life has a nasty way of sending you more lessons. Best to listen to the universe while it whispers before it has to shout.

If you've been working your way through these chapters and are actively applying these questions and strategies to your specific situation, this is the part where it really gets exciting. Now is when you look at your unique circumstances and

> "Get the message out of the mess".
> ~Marion Grobb Finkelstein

accept the gift that life is offering you. The gems are buried in the previous step where you identified how things could be worse--that's why that exercise is so important.

Each of these steps builds on the other. While it's not necessary to follow them strictly in sequential order, you may find it useful to do so. Feel free to hop back and forth and revisit steps as you please. Make this system work for you. Adapt it as your require. As long as you cover each step thoroughly, collectively they will move you down the path to build your resilience, shift your attitude to one that is more positive, and transform your outcome to one that more closely resembles what you want.

> "... never minimize your loss, make light of your suffering, or downplay the severity of your challenge".
> ~Marion Grobb Finkelstein

When exploring your gift and the lessons learned, including your gratitude about how it could be worse, remember that the intent is never to minimize your loss, make light of your suffering, or downplay the severity of your challenge. Quite the contrary.

The very deliberate steps leading up to this point look backward at events that have already happened and how to reframe them, whereas this step of unwrapping your gift and the additional steps we will soon explore, are forward-looking and designed to help you turn your ship around and steer toward your goals.

How to unwrap your gift

Now I invite you to grab that list you created of all the ways your situation could be worse. We're going to revisit each item you thought of or wrote down and, one by one, flip them into positives. Each of those points is a gift you have been given and this exercise will help you unwrap it. Take a moment and focus on your situation.

Let me share an example to help you better understand how this step of identifying the gift really works.

Unpacking Debbie's divorce gift

In the previous chapter, we looked at the case of Debbie's divorce. We talked about how difficult this was for her. We learned about her pain and her sense of tremendous loss. Debbie progressed to the point that she was able to describe her own role that contributed to the ultimate ending of the marriage, and to do so without pointing fingers or blame at herself or others. She exercised her ability to look at her situation and describe it without being emotionally charged. In the process, Debbie unearths many ways that her situation could be worse and is now one hop closer to discovering her gift.

One of ways Debbie noted that her situation could be worse is if she had no friends or family to support her. She goes on to state that "at least" she has a great support system. So what's the gift, what did she learn from this aspect? She now knows who she can really count on and who will come forward to actively support her during difficult times.

See how we flipped what she may *not* have had into recognizing something that she did, using the "at least" technique? Then we took it a step further to determine what she learned and in doing so, unwrapped her gift. We can do that for every item she wrote about how her situation could be worse. You can do that for your list too.

If you process information very visually and sequentially, you could do this exercise in chart form. Here's an excerpt of Debbie's list showing what she had originally written down as to how it could be worse, the "at least" statement, and then the most recent step of flipping each of those negative points into acknowledging the gifts that she has been given.

Debbie's "how could it be worse"	At least ...	The gift (i.e., what I learned)
The bad relationship could have continued for a longer period	At least ... The bad relationship only lasted for a short time and not my whole life	I learned that I'm stronger than I thought I was.
... he could have had an affair and flaunted it	At least ... He was discreet and didn't publicly humiliate me	I realize that his actions are his alone and don't define me.
... if we hadn't had nine wonderful years	At least ... We had nine happy years together	I got to experience more happy years than some people ever get to have
... I could be left destitute	At least ... I have financial resources and he isn't taking everything	I learned how to advocate for myself to ensure my financial security
... if I had no support system	At least ... I am encircled by a group of friends and family	I know who I can really count on and found support in places I never knew I had

In all the gifts mentioned in Debbie's example, you'll note that each step in the process builds on the other. This systematic approach of handling a difficult situation is akin to chipping away at a marble block to unearth the beautiful piece of art hiding below. That's your gift.

Using a chart may help you gather and organize your thoughts. If that approach works for you, use it. If not, if you enjoy a more less linear approach to your thinking, feel free to simply brainstorm a list of your gifts. The following examples will give you an idea of how this informal and non-linear approach looks. Neither method is right or wrong, just different. Use the one that appeals to you, feels more natural, and best fits how you process information. Both will lead you to your gifts.

You may be wondering if the *Finkelstein Factor*™ and *Flip It Formula*™ can be used for civic matters and public policies. Yes, absolutely! This system is useful in personal struggles or professionally challenging situations. The process applies and is equally effective, regardless of what the circumstance is that is you're managing.

Here's a perfect example of a real-life situation. If you've ever engaged in real estate issues, this one will resonate with you.

Goodbye Golf Course

Several years ago, a golf course in a popular Ontario city sold parcels of its peripheral lands to a developer who, in turn, built homes and sold them to more than one hundred individual families. All of the homeowners paid handsome premiums to live in what they were told was a prestigious golf course community, some investing significant supplemental fees to enjoy the additional benefit of golf course view.

Fast forward six years and the golf course owners sell all eighteen holes and the remaining additional lands to offshore foreign investors. The new golf course owners hire a consulting company that hosts a public meeting to announce their plans of replacing the golf course with more houses and townhomes.

The current homeowners, especially those located on holes offering spectacular and expensive golf course views, are distraught. They fear their real estate investments, upscale neighborhood, and the lifestyle that they bought into are at risk.

The new golf course owners are proposing removing these premium backyard views and replacing them with back-to-back houses. No more lakes and trees, just views of other people's backyards. They require zoning amendments to proceed with any development plans and the homeowners intend to fight tooth and nail.

So what's the gift from this volatile volcano of a situation? If you were a homeowner on this property, what would you say? Remember, the gift is all about what you're learning. What would you discover that you didn't know before? What additional skills would you gain that you didn't have before? Upon reflection, you may acknowledge your list of gifts as including some of the following:

- Uniting neighbours to battle against a common unwanted situation bands together neighbours who have never had occasion to meet before, forging friendships and relationships that otherwise would never have happened;
- Neighbours display leadership qualities and expertise others never realized they had building newfound respect and acknowledgement of expertise and skills;
- Individuals stretch their comfort zones and learn to assert themselves, speak up, and approach stakeholders and decision-makers to get their voice heard;
- This situation presents an opportunity for homeowners to learn about municipal politics and how to influence policy and zoning decisions;
- Homeowners feel empowered by working together.

Maybe it's not a zoning situation you're grappling with but chances are you've dealt with or are dealing with some sort of change in your life. It's most difficult when you feel that change is being imposed upon you. The key in this real estate example is the lesson of exerting your influence and feeling like you have a venue to get your voice heard.

More difficult is a situation where you feel you don't have due process or an opportunity to have your say. Even if that is the case, look for the gift. It's there.

Remember how I explained this book was in large part inspired by my husband, Steve, and his many somewhat funny trials and tribulations? I say, "funny" because Steve has this magic and well honed ability to find humour in the most remote places. It's truly a gift. I believe that the shorter the time between when an incident occurs and when you're able to laugh at the craziness of it, the more developed your funny bone. The goal is to make that time lapse as short as possible. If you're going to laugh someday, let that day be today.

The *Finkelstein Factor*™ isn't just about things going wrong--it's about recovery time and rebounding. My husband must be made of rubber because he bends to the situation and bounces back quickly. Take the following example.

Steve's tightened tendon

When Steve is in his late forties, it starts off as an annoying bump in his right palm. Being a right-handed trumpet player, he is very aware of it and its slow and steady growth. Ten years later, that bump begins to interfere with his hand movements and ability to spread his fingers wide. He finds his ability to push down the trumpet keys quickly slightly diminished. Partly out of concern and partly out of curiosity, he seeks medical opinion and discovers that he has a tightened tendon that will only get worse.

Doctors advise Steve that, eventually, his hand will close almost completely, leaving only his thumb protruding outward With his quirky sense of humour, Steve raises his bent hand and quips, "Well doc, the good news is that soon, I'll be able to go hitchhiking". Yup, that right there, is the Finkelstein Factor™, *the ability to bounce back from adversity.*

You may be asking, what on earth is the gift?

One day Steve is listening to a medical talk show and the doctor is discussing tightening tendons when he divulges something that leaves Steve riveted. The doctor explains that this tightened tendon in the hand is unique to those of Viking heritage. In fact, these nodules in the hands are called, "Viking disease". Steve can't believe it! He loves this interesting fact about his lineage and begins researching his condition with renewed enthusiasm as he imagines his forefathers being Vikings. Had it not been for this medical situation, he would never have known to connect his present with this very distant past. That's a gift. Steve having this condition led him to this gift of discovering a piece of his heritage.

Steve find another gift in another story he can tell and joke he can crack related to his latest discovery. He figures that under those glorious Viking horned helmets, they surely must have worn yarmulkes. Who knew?

Let's revisit the issue of my cervical spine challenges. I am excited to share with you the gifts that this challenge gave me.

Marion's cervical spine issues--the gift

Since my cervical spine issues I experienced several years ago, I often think about the gifts this episode in my life gave me. There are many. Here's a snippet of some of the things I learned and came to realize during this time. Some of these gifts are proof, evidence, and confirmation of what I have always believed. Some of the other gifts are newfound gems I would never have known had I not lived this experience:

- *I now have a deepened respect and compassion for people who live with chronic pain;*
- *I learn how pain can morph a personality, and that gives me more patience with those who are suffering;*
- *I learn what a difference a little bit of help from others can make;*
- *I learn to self-care and listen to my body more.*

This really isn't an example restricted to illness. It's about finding the gift, the lesson, in any adversity you're facing. What have *you* learned from yours? What have you discovered about yourself or others? What's your gift?

When it comes to acknowledging the gift adversity gives, I find myself wandering back to a familiar story I heard years ago. It vividly demonstrates how challenges come with lessons, and those lessons are precious gifts.

Moses's misery

It's 1914 in Shawinigan, Quebec. Families typically have many children and traditional values. Wealthy Canadian homes are being introduced to electricity, Robert Borden is Canada's Prime Minister, and our country is bracing itself to launch into World War

One, the bloodiest conflict in Canadian history claiming the lives of more than 60,000 Canadians.

Against this backdrop, Moses is five years old and the apple of his father's eye. He is touted around proudly by his dad, Joshua Charles who holds a senior management position in a nearby factory. Joshua brings little Moses to the front lines to introduce him to his staff. He tells anyone who will listen that this is his only son of six children. Moses feels loved and cherished, because he truly is.

One day, Moses peers into his father's home office and is awestruck to see his papa lift a heavy oak desk and dash it against the wall. In his child's mind, he believes his father is surely a superhero with incredible strength. Shortly after that, his mother breaks the news to the family that his father is very ill. Quickly, he succumbs to what Moses learns in later years, is meningitis. As an adult and in retrospect, Moses understands that his father's unnatural strength was spawned by unthinkable pain. At the time, however, all he knows is that he is now without his hero.

The following two years bring with them more tragedy. Being the era before antibiotics, consumption (now known as tuberculosis) robs Moses of three siblings and worst of all, his beloved mother. Now orphaned, Moses and his remaining two sisters go to live with their aunt, uncle and four cousins. Even though the children are from two families, they are raised as siblings. They don't call him cousin Moses--they call him brother Moses. Me? I just called him Dad.

I can't think of life's gifts without thinking of my father's story. It was in a rare father-daughter hour that he shared it with me and it prompted me to ask, "Whatever did you learn from so much misery in such a short time at such a young age?" I was asking about his gift.

Without skipping a beat, my father responded with one word--empathy. He learned empathy. That was the gift. My father lived his life looking through that lens of empathy and that was both the gift he got and the gift he gave to world. What's yours?

There are many types of gifts

Once you get used to recognizing the gifts, you can see them just about everywhere. They come in all different shapes, sizes, and types. What you see as a gift may not be what someone else sees and vice versa. Your gifts are personalized to you and founded on your perceptions, mindset, and what you need and value.

Discover your existing strengths

In general, discovering your gift involves unearthing strengths you forget you have. For example, dealing with a loss of any sort requires you to dig down and find reserves that were always there and overlooked. Whether it's the loss of a loved one through death, divorce, or disease, you uncover the fortitude to carry on that you always had. Think about the Wizard of Oz and the gifts the wizard gave the travellers. They were all things they already had, just never realized they did.

In recognizing your existing strengths, you unearth skills you may not have used in years that are instrumental to you coping. Now is your chance to let those skills and strengths resurface and shine once again. You used them before. Dust them off and use them again.

Develop new skills

Pushing past your comfort zone into new areas stretches and

grows aspects of yourself that now become new resources. You learn new skills and things about yourself you never realized. Suppose your job gets cut and you end up considering career tracks you previously had overlooked or always wanted to follow and didn't know how. Now is your chance to grab that opportunity and start anew. Your gift may be that you master new skills and become a rejuvenated you.

Create options

Your gift provides you with the occasion to think creatively and outside the box that you or others may have placed you in.

Perhaps your dreams of becoming an actor in the TV show you auditioned for, haven't come to pass. What's the gift? You get to create options, new ways, to get what you need that you wouldn't have explored otherwise. Now you get to stretch your wings elsewhere--community theatre, commercials, or volunteer at your local cablevision. Maybe you express your creativity by producing or directing instead of acting. Perhaps you write a screenplay or script for a local theatre production. You build your team of supporters in another way. You express yourself and have your need met through other vehicles. It's not failing--it's succeeding in a different way.

You forge talents, relationships, and alliances that otherwise would have eluded you. In turning on your creative juices, you discover solutions you never realized existed, and in doing so, you find your gift.

How to word it

Once you've had a chance to enunciate what it is you learned from your experience, you can cement that lesson using the following sentence structure:

> "Had it not been for this experience (NAME WHAT IT WAS), I wouldn't know/realize/be able to _____ _____ (NAME what you learned about yourself or others, what new skills you gained or realized)"

In the stories above, here are some ways that the gifts could be presented. These are offered as examples only. When you're defining your own gifts, use the words that feel most comfortable to you. Word it so it fits you and is authentic. Make it your own.

> "Had it not been for the divorce, I would never have known how strong I am and able to survive and thrive on my own."

> "Because of our community fighting to keep the golf course, I've forged new friendships with neighbours I didn't really know before."

> "When my hand tendons started tightening, it gave me the chance to explore medical options and really appreciate my hand mobility while I have it. Plus, I learned I have Viking heritage, cool!"

> "Living through the painful experience of cervical spine issues, I now have an intimate understanding of and greater compassion for those who suffer from chronic pain."

> "Losing my parents and siblings when I was so young taught me to be empathetic toward others and refrain from judgment. Everyone has a story."

Being able to see your gift requires switching off your emotional self and turning on your logic. You already have this ability to be rational and make fact-based decisions. You've done it many times in your life.

For example, last time you made a big-ticket purchase such as a car or house, you likely considered the financial investment, the payments required, whether you could reasonably afford this purchase, how many months or years the payments will last, how long you expect to use the item you are buying, and a multitude of other pragmatic considerations. These are all logic-based decisions. That's not to say that your heart doesn't come into play; of course it does. It's only to point out that you already have a keen sense of logic in your decision-making and you can draw upon this existing strength to complete the exercise of finding your hidden gift. If you don't naturally have this ability, now is your opportunity to hone it. Another gift!

When you're in a tempest and your world is turned upside down, it's important to return to the center of your logical self so you can harmonize the emotionally charged feelings with hardcore logic. Your gift is ready, and even though it may take a bit of time to find and unwrap it, I assure you, it exists.

Chapter 6 recap

- Your gift is what you learn, so be sure to get the message out of the mess;
- Focus on your gifts to discover existing strengths, develop new skills, and create options you never would have known you had without experiencing this challenge;
- Word it by acknowledging what you now know or can do that you didn't before your difficult episode.

WHAT'S THE GIFT?

You're at the place now where you can look more objectively at your challenge. You have the questions and exercises to pull the hurt, lessons, and positives from an otherwise terrible situation. You're ready to turn your attention to the future.

CHAPTER 7

STEP 2, Q4: WHAT WILL YOU CHANGE IN FUTURE?

Move knowledge to action

One aspect of your challenge and, in fact, of your life, that you will never be able to change, is the past. What has happened has happened. No amount of wishing, pining, or complaining will throw you back in time to relive that moment. What you said or did can never be taken back. No matter how hard you may try, you aren't able to unring that bell.

The one thing you can completely change is your future. The first step in the *Flip It Formula*™ is backward-looking and about acknowledging your loss. The following first three questions in step two also require you to be reflective and focused on the past. Now, in question four, is the time to switch gears and move

Flip It Formula™

STEP 1: Acknowledge the loss

STEP 2: Ask four flippin' questions
- 1) What is **my role**?
- 2) How could it be **worse**?
- 3) What's the **gift**?
- 4) What will I **change in future**?

into the future. You can't do this by looking in the rearview mirror, so no more backward gazing. Although it's important to know where you've come from, it's far more important to know where you're going.

This struggle you may be currently living is an opportunity to choose a different path, to change your default response, and to create outcomes that are far more satisfying. Every step you take, every decision you make, every word you speak or choose not to, can move you in the direction you want to go. Being mindful of your mindset and your reactions is the key. Take those lessons from the past, apply them to your present, and change your future.

Your lessons are transferable

The skills you unearth during this process are transferable. This is why the steps of defining the deep hurt you endure, the hard-earned lessons learned, and ultimately the gifts and treasures you find buried deep inside you, are essential. You don't want to live that pain again so remembering how much it hurt is a huge motivator to ensure you avoid it in future. Recognizing and *applying* the lessons you learn along the way will help you create your new future.

They apply to other situations

The exact same challenge you're currently tackling may never raise its ugly head again for as long as you live. However, you will likely have similar ones where your lessons learned and your gifts will apply. For example, that episode with a bully boss you dealt with may never recur with another supervisor, though what you learned prepares you to more competently manage a bully employee, colleague or client. It gives you skills for your personal life and to deal with a bully partner, parent, or child, or to assert yourself in other situations requiring you to speak up and take a stand.

They apply to other people

You might not be able to apply the valuable gems you've unearthed to *your* life. However, what you've learned may help *others*. It is in this spirit that I share all the steps and processes in this book. My sincere hope is that what I've learned along the way may help you. Even though we may not have lived exactly the same experiences, the principles of what I share will still be of use to you.

Wouldn't life be shallow if you couldn't get anything from your pain, skills, and gifts and help someone in the process? Learning, sharing, and sparing yourself and others unnecessary pain can render purpose and meaning to your challenges and experience. I know that with certainty because it does for me.

You can use the lessons and skills learned to help others.

The concept of limited energy

Consider the concept of what I call, "limited energy". You only have a certain amount of energy in your body. How you spend it is up to you. I invite you to be mindful of where you direct your resources. Instead of using up energy in areas that won't change your situation, such as worry, anger, guilt, or regret, why not consciously decide to direct those efforts toward finding productive options and solutions? Remember, you show the world what you value by how you spend your resources. What are you spending your limited energy on and is it getting you results? If not, you may want to shift your attention.

Apply your lessons in future

This book offers a systematic series of questions to assist you in adjusting your mindset and considering the impact of your typical default responses. We're going to take a peek at some of your previous work and the questions you visited and use your homework to build our path forward.

Several chapters ago, you pondered the question, "What is my role?". You're going to use that list now. Here's how.

On a sheet of paper, draw a line down the middle. On the left-hand side, list all the things you think, say, or do that contribute to you creating your difficult situation. On the right, flip it. That is, for each action you note that worsens your situation and provokes your unfortunate outcome, what's the opposite you could do? Write it down. What do you routinely think or say that continues the cycle? Flip those too and describe in your right-hand column what you could think or say instead. All these flipped items listed on the right side of your page are your new plan of attack.

Let's look at a workplace example we talked about earlier.

Boss keeps you waiting

Let's use the example of the boss who seems to constantly keep you waiting for meetings. You linger in his outer office as he takes calls or works behind his closed door, oblivious to the impact his actions are having on you. In the chart below, in the column on the left are some of the ways you may have knowingly or unknowingly contributed to creating or continuing the unsatisfactory results you're getting. The column on the right suggests how you could flip your behaviour to produce different and more favorable outcomes in the future. As you read through them, see what you might be able to apply if you were in this difficult situation.

MY ROLE ... (What I may be doing that is creating or continuing this situation)	IN FUTURE ... (Flip it, change what I do to change my result)
Spend my energy and spinning my wheels getting ticked off, insulted, and feeling discounted	Embrace this quiet waiting time as a chance to catch up on reading or working on files I now bring with me
I tolerate this situation and have never told my boss how much it bothers me and affects my operational effectiveness	I will change the situation by checking with my boss a few minutes before we meet to confirm that he's still running on time, or to reschedule at his convenience
I complain to other colleagues about the situation and find solace that I'm not alone	I'll stop complaining and start creating a new reality. I'll share tips I use to manage the situation with my colleagues and ask them what they do to manage.

This next step of what you will do in future isn't only about acknowledging what you've learned, it's about *applying* it. With this roadmap of questions and exercises in the previous chapters, you are adding tools to your coping kit. You are resetting your mindset and adjusting how you see and manage your situation. As you look toward your future, identifying behaviours you control and will modify is your chance to change your outcomes.

In addition or instead of using a chart, you may choose to ponder your future actions with a less structured format. If this style suits you better, the following questions will get your creative juices flowing. Focus your thinking to look forward, and generate a plethora of ways to flip your current actions into more constructive ones that will support your desired outcomes. These flipped actions will aid you in taking what you've learned in the past into the future to tackle the next challenge awaiting you around the corner:

- In a similar situation, what will you do differently in the future?
- What did you do before that undermined your objectives and will now consciously *stop* doing?
- What will you do *more* of that will move you toward desired results?
- What will you do *less* of that will move you toward desired results?
- What new skills will you be sure to apply?
- What options will you exercise that you previously didn't realize you had?
- What self-talk will you be sure to use?

Using this approach, let's take another office-related example we touched on earlier. It's one that may sound very familiar to you or someone you know.

Betty's budget cuts

Betty is a project manager of many years. Recently, her organization has been restructured resulting in drastic reductions to her operating budgets, yet her annual goals aren't reduced at all. In fact, she feels that the higher-ups have cut so much of the proverbial fat they are now cutting into the muscle.

Going through the Flip It Formula™ process, Betty describes what she feels she has lost, her role, how it could be worse, and the gifts she's gaining. She manages to look outside her traditional thinking and develops options of getting sponsors to supplement her project's lost budget.

Now, let's skip to how she's going to move the knowledge she's gained to action. As she moves forward with this and future projects, she will do these things differently:

- *Give her supervisor periodic updates of project milestones versus waiting almost until completion;*
- *Track her new partners' degree of satisfaction from the newly formed relationships;*
- *Leverage her experience with sponsorship to develop similar partners for her other projects;*
- *Speak at conferences about her challenge, how she handled it, and share sponsorship techniques her colleagues will find useful;*
- *Assert herself and her accomplishments more readily.*

Betty has carried the lessons forward. What lessons and gifts have you gained and will *you* use in the future?

You are the creator of your own reality

You don't control what life rolls in your direction but you, one hundred percent, control how you respond. In other words, you are the creator of your own reality. So stop complaining, start creating. You are responsible for your own outcomes. That's wonderful news and brings with it two facts:

1. The good news is that if you don't like your reality, you have the power to change it;
2. The bad news is that now you have no one to blame.

This book is written on the premise of assuming responsibility and not wasting your limited energy on finger-pointing to yourself or others. You are an artist painting your life. Make it joyous.

How to word it

Time to put it all together. Incorporating on some of the previous questions and techniques, this is how you could explain to yourself and others your way forward, how you will move to action what you have learned to change your outcomes and the results you want.

(STATE the loss)_____. At least / the good news is / thank goodness _____ (state the upside, the gift). Next time I will do / see / say / think (STATE what you will do differently in future) OR ... Now, (STATE your new course of action)

In the examples we've used above, the way forward statement could read as follows:

"I was losing a lot of time and energy waiting for my boss as he took other calls and delayed our meeting time. At least I learned quickly how to use that quiet time productively and now I bring files with me to read as I wait. I find that I actually appreciate having uninterrupted moments to focus".

"My budget is being cut and I'm losing my enthusiasm for my job. At least I still have a job and all my amazing staff members. As I move forward, I'm going to tap into their creative minds to brainstorm potential sponsors and strategic alliances we could forge to create win-wins".

Whether you write it down or just think about it, how would you word *your* way forward? What action or inaction will you change? Identify how what you think, say, and do contributes to your role, because now you have the power to change them.

Chapter 7 recap

- Your lessons are transferable to other situations and other people;
- Knowledge is only powerful when you move it to action;
- Flip your role into action items to move forward;
- You are the creator of your own reality.

We've covered a lot of material to help you work through a difficult situation, flip your mindset and outcome to a positive one, and to create the reality you want and deserve. There is another very critical step in the process and that's what we're going to touch on next. It's one of the toughest things to do and it's all about how to let go.

CHAPTER 8

STEP 3: LET GO
Release the pain and move forward

Having reached this point in the book, I truly hope you have participated in and gained from all the exercises. Even if you haven't actually done the exercises and answered all the questions, the examples show you how you can do so when you're ready.

You have worked through the system, and gotten everything you possibly could from your negative situation. You have succeeded in naming your loss, validating your hurt, defining your role, and pulling the message from your mess. The next step is to let go. But how?

We all know letting go of pain and hurt makes sense, so why doesn't everyone do it? It's because your head is telling you one thing, yet no one is showing your heart *how* ... until now.

PRINCIPLE OF LETTING GO: Hanging on to the past keeps you tethered to the ground

Hanging on to the past and pain prevents you from propelling yourself forward and flying high. You just can't do it. It's against the laws of physics. A hot air balloon can only elevate and move forward when its ties to the earth are released. You simply can't move forward into the future when you are hanging on to the past.

Remember when you were a child, playing on the monkey bars? Think back to that moment. You love gripping those rungs and, arm by arm, swinging yourself forward. Oh, that feeling of freedom and achievement as you reach the other side! Then you hop off, jump down, and go running back to the beginning to do it all again. Without realizing it, you are learning a very key principle in life: You can't grab the next bar in front of you until you release the one behind.

That metaphor perfectly illustrates the principle of letting go.

Whenever I think about letting go, I'm reminded of the following story. I hope it resonates with you as much as it does with me and gives you insight into the people, places, and things that are holding you stationary and preventing you from moving forward.

Moving Maggie

A good friend of mine--let's say her name is Maggie--is in the midst of moving from her beautifully appointed three-bedroom Ottawa family home to a much smaller empty-nest condo in downtown Toronto. It is a huge lifestyle adjustment. She and her husband are leaving the home where they raised their two children who are now fully grown and on their own. These walls embrace more than twenty years of family memories. Steve and I share in those memories, with many dinners, after-golf beverages, and celebrations under this roof.

One day, as I am helping Maggie prepare for a huge garage sale, I look around the basement noticing price tags on all their once-cherished items. A twinge of sadness creeps over me and I verbalize what I think might be Maggie's loss, suggesting, "It must be very difficult for you to say goodbye to all these things."

Maggie replies with words that guide me still, years later. She wisely advises, "Marion, these are anchors that are weighing me down. It's absolutely liberating to let go."

That's it! It was like a splash of cold water on my face: Letting go is emancipating.

PRINCIPLE OF LETTING GO: It takes as much energy to hang on to the past as it does to move into the future

Think back to the monkey bar example. Imagine yourself firmly gripping the bar above you with both hands. You soon learn that if you maintain your firm and static hold on the bars, all your energy is used staying put. It takes great strength to keep those bars tight in your hands and support your weight without moving. Over time, you could spend perhaps even more energy doing this than it would have taken to move forward.

Remember the principle of limited energy? You only have so much energy in your body and how you spend it is your choice and determines your results. You have the ability to decide whether you will spend your energy staying mired in the past or use it to let go and propel yourself forward. Like all the steps, strategies, and tactics I suggest in this book, that choice is strictly up to you. I hope you choose the right one--the one that helps you grow and actualize.

Forgiveness is a gift you give yourself

Hanging on to pain, hate, anger, and regret takes energy. Releasing it gives relief, love, joy, and appreciation. Part of letting go is about forgiving yourself and others for whatever roles you or they may have played, knowingly or unknowingly, in creating your difficult time.

When you're able to overcome those emotions, you'll be able to see yourself and the person or circumstance that offended you dispassionately and objectively. Instead of feeling anger and resentment toward yourself or others, this approach allows you to experience compassion for yourself and others because you'll see those who have offended you as being stuck whereas you are free. Releasing the emotional charge of your situation frees you to experience a new reality that now begins to unfold. You've moved on and can now see how this new way of looking at difficult situations and experiences helps to push you forward and mold your life and reality. Forgiveness is a surprising byproduct.

Mastering this skill of removing emotion from an explosive situation requires practice and sometimes, a great deal of time. It also requires a process to systematically walk you through the landmines, and that is exactly the purpose of this book. By consistently practicing the steps and asking the questions this books outlines, you will soon find yourself thinking and reacting differently when things go wrong. Situations that used to set you off in a negative downward spiral will no longer hold that power over you.

Forgiveness is something you do, not for the other person or persons involved: It's a gift you give yourself. Acknowledge and then forgive yourself for your contribution to any negative energy you may have held or given. Forgive yourself, forgive others.

Forgiving someone doesn't give them licence to abuse you. Forgiving doesn't mean you forget. Forgiving doesn't mean you're weak. It means you take the lesson and move forward. Perhaps it's no coincidence that the word *forgiveness* begins with the letter "f" and so does the gift it gives you--freedom. Don't do it for them. Do it for you.

How to let go

You deserve to live your life to the fullest, leave the pain behind, and step into your future without guilt or regret. You want to let go of that specific hurtful or energy-sucking situation. Let me show you how.

For many years and through a variety of life challenges, I fought to crack the code of *how to let go*. It can be incredibly difficult. Through trials and errors of my own and feedback from hundreds of my clients, I crystallized what I learned into six salient questions. What took me about a lifetime to learn, I share with you readily with the hope that it spares you losing any more joy from your life.

Let go guide, Q1: Do you control it?

Think about a recent challenge in your life, perhaps something you're currently experiencing and having difficulty moving past, something you would like to release. Ask yourself honestly if you have complete control over the situation and all its variables.

Let Go Guide™

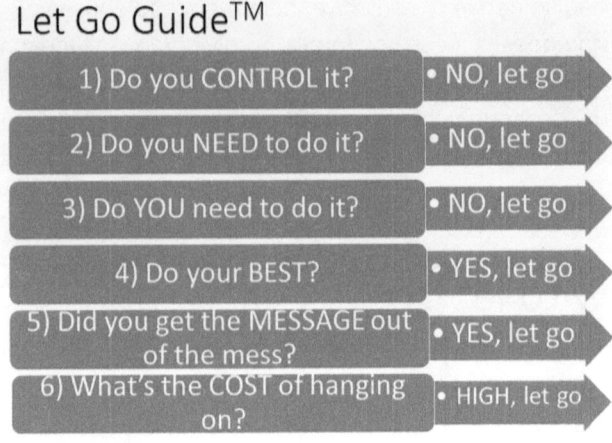

You may control your action and do the right thing, yet how the other person responds is completely up to him or her. Remind yourself of this fact when things don't turn out quite the way you'd hoped. You don't control how someone responds. Continue doing what you know is the correct and honorable behaviour, even though it may not be reciprocated or received in the spirit in which it was intended. And realize that you may not control the unsatisfactory and perhaps unwarranted response you receive.

Here's an example of determining if you personally control "it", whatever the it may be. In this case, it's making funeral arrangements and reaching out to an estranged family member.

Fern's funeral formalities

Fern's father passes away and the funeral arrangements are taken care of by family members. Fern oversees the procedures and even though he hasn't spoken to his sibling in years, he knows that the time to do so has arrived. He dreads the encounter but with respect to his deceased father, picks up the phone and speaks personally to his brother, not knowing whether the response will be civil or icy cold. He finds solace in recognizing that he doesn't control his brother's reactions, so he's letting go of the worry associated with how his brother may react.

In asking the question, "*Do you control it?*", Fern feels a release. He knows that the answer is *no* and in doing so, acknowledges that hanging on to his worry serves no purpose. No matter how much he worries or thinks about it, he can't change his brother's reaction, whatever it will be. Fern chooses what he believes to be the high road, initiates contact, and reaches out to his brother. He is now ready to let go of this concern and move forward.

Epilogue: his brother also does what he considers to be the right thing, and responds very constructively to his brother's call. Both men honour their deceased parent in doing so.

In your situation, do you completely control the outcome or someone else's response? If you honestly answer no, maybe it's time for you to let go of that worry. Not sure? Continue with the next five questions and you will have greater clarity still.

Let go guide, Q2: Do you *need* to do it?

Is the worry, anger, or negative emotion you're harbouring now centred around an action you feel you *need* to do? In other words, will what you're considering largely change your life for the positive? Is there a good chance that this event or action will have a huge impact on your life?

If you answer *no*, that's your clue to move on.

Maybe your challenge doesn't deserve a great deal of energy or more of your resources. It could be you don't really *need* to do it, it's not a life-changer, and stewing over it is draining you physically, financially or emotionally. Remember, you don't *need* to do anything: You *choose* to or not. You may decide to let it go.

Perfect Penny

Penny is a stay-home mom and prides herself on keeping a perfect house. She has a place for everything and everything in its place. When company is expected, she routinely dusts and cleans like there is no tomorrow. Pillows are plumped, air fresheners plugged in, and cut flowers adorn her counter.

When her children start school full-time, Penny takes on a challenging job and finds herself working long and tiring hours. She can't seem to muster the energy to engage in her normal household chores. The dusting and cleaning that used to bring her great satisfaction now hang over her like a dreaded chore. It's one more thing to do in an already time-pressed day. She notices with utter disgust that dust has gathered on her baseboards. She sighs at the pile of dirty laundry screaming for her attention.

Penny asks herself the question, "Do I have to do the housework?" She decides the answer is no. She doesn't need or want to maintain the household the way she used to. She reasons, in the big scheme of things, her children and partner will remember her spending time with them, not if the table is wiped or counter crumb-free. Penny rids herself of the perfection bug and gives herself permission to join the rest of us mere mortals. She lets go.

What are you hanging on to that no longer makes a big difference to you? What used to be a pleasure and is now a pain? Are you dealing with a disappointment of some sort that is serving as an emotional vampire and sucking you dry? If you've determined the missed opportunity you're mourning won't impact your future in any significant way, then perhaps it's time to let it go.

You may let go completely or choose to redefine that dream or standard. Continuing a behaviour or holding on to a picture in your mind of how the world should be, may be draining you of your precious energy you could be spending on people and areas of your life that would bring you much more satisfaction.

Letting go is liberating, allows you to reframe your expectations, and frees you up to grab new opportunities you didn't see before.

Let go guide, Q3: Do *you* need to do it?

You may be hanging on tooth and nail to a behaviour, project, or task you enjoy doing simply for that reason--you enjoy doing it. Someone else could do it quite competently but you don't want to release your talons. Sound familiar?

Let's take a look at a workplace example of someone finding it difficult to let go of a pleasurable task.

Video Vicki

Vicki loves her job as an advertising creative manager. Having come up through the ranks, she's familiar with all the steps required to produce a television commercial. One of the tasks she really enjoys is auditioning the talent. Even though her account representatives reporting to her typically perform this task, Vicki insists that her they include her in this process.

Under a tight deadline, a staff member approaches Vicki and asks to carry out the auditions in her absence while she's on business travel. He does this to respect deadlines and ensure that the client's ad is produced in time for airing.

Vicki's first gut reaction is a hard no. Then she pauses and asks the sobering questions, "Do I need to do it? Does it need to be me?" Upon some reflection, Vicki admits that she's been hanging on to this piece of the puzzle far too long. She realizes that there's an opportunity cost to her performing this function that could easily be delegated to others. Her doing all the auditions is robbing her of time to manage bigger issues for which she is uniquely qualified. In addition, she comes to recognize that she's actually stunting her staff's growth potential and confidence by not allowing them to assume this role.

Vicki decides it's time to let go and delegate. She doesn't need to do this task as her staff is very able. She lets go and lets them.

Does any of this resonate with you? Whether in your personal or professional life, you likely find yourself in situations where you are spending resources--your time, energy, money--on tasks and projects that others could quite easily do.

Perhaps what's holding you back from delegating is fear. You may be worried that others won't do the task as well as you, or will do it differently. It's going to bother you every time you look at their results knowing that you would have done it another way. Your fear isn't holding back only you--it's holding back other people who want to contribute, feel valuable, and would appreciate having an opportunity to tackle that challenge.

Consider, for example, managers who hinder the progress of employees to problem solve or have critical thinking skills because they take over. Or parents who don't allow their children to take measured risks and handle tasks. Part of letting go is acknowledging that everyone does things differently. Many roads lead to Rome. Some are straight and fast, others take a scenic route. As long as deadlines are respected, does it matter if someone does it a different way? (HINT: the answer is *no*). Just think how letting go is freeing you up for more exciting adventures while helping others grow.

You will often find that others will help you achieve your goals and willingly carry the torch in the relay, only if you let it go.

Let Go Guide, Q4: Did you do your best?

When you step back and reflect upon your difficult situation, can you look yourself in the mirror and know that you truly did the best you could? You may have given it that good old college effort, using all the skills, knowledge, and emotional energy you had at the time, and missed the mark. It happens. If you answer *yes, you tried your best given your skills and circumstances at the time*, you may have earned your ticket to let go.

Take a peek at how this principle plays out during a job interview.

Ingrid's interview

Ingrid is considering a career change. Although she enjoys her position as an executive assistant, she's interested in moving into an event planner position within her organization. She applies for an opening, gets an interview, and thinks she's done quite well. A week later, she finds out she isn't the successful candidate.

At first, she's so disappointed she wants to give up her event planning path. She feels like a failure and is embarrassed to tell her colleagues the results of the competition. She judges herself harshly and silently chides her lack of knowledge. She wonders if the outfit she wore to the interview gave the right impression. Maybe that time she laughed aloud wasn't well received? She bets her answers weren't as good as the panel was expecting.

Then she asks herself the question, did I do my best? She thinks about how she spent hours studying. She remembers how she spoke to an event planner she knows to get an appreciation for the challenges of the job. She anticipated potential questions and prepared answers in advance. She enrolled in an event management program at her local college. She showed her resume to a few trusted colleagues for their suggestions. She mentioned her career desires to her supervisor who offered a few tips.

Yes, Ingrid feels she had done her best. With that acknowledgement, she is able to move past her disappointment, hold her head high, and look forward to applying again for her perfect job.

In the example I just shared with you, Ingrid at first whips herself to the point that she is uncertain that she will even pursue her passion. Have you ever surrendered to discouragement? You feel beaten up and your confidence is shaken. Find comfort and energy in the fact that you did or are doing your best, given the circumstances. Give yourself permission to release self judgement. Be proud of your efforts, regardless of the outcome. Chances are you did and accomplished much more than many ever would.

Let go of the judgement and disappointment, not the dream.

Let go guide, Q5: Did you get the message out of the mess?

We touched on the topic of pulling a message from the mess in an earlier chapter. Every misfortune provides an opportunity to learn; make sure you grab it. If you miss the message, life will send these learning opportunities again and again until you get it. It can be a painful and draining journey when you see the same misfortune occurring over and over. It's best to catch the lesson first time around.

Sarcastic Cindy

When she's really stressed, Cindy drips sarcasm over her unsuspecting recipients. Instead of responding factually, she snaps out sarcastic jabs that are often unappreciated. Her colleagues perceive her as being difficult to work with and argumentative. Her partner says she's quick-witted ... to a fault.

Cindy receives her annual appraisal and her boss notes that her enviable work performance is marred by her sarcasm. He offers several specific examples he's witnessed. He recognizes that it may be her attempt to cope and add humour to a situation, and suggests that it's not working. He opines that sarcasm is veiled contempt and to be avoided.

Cindy is devastated. She's never been told this before. She believes her comments were demonstrating her cleverness. Sure, they were laced with a sting, and she saw that as part of the fun. She is wrong.

After the initial shock, Cindy steps back to consider her boss's review of her performance. She remembers the examples he gave her when she used sarcasm which had been perceived as a weapon against others. She is now convinced this behaviour is undermining the results she hopes to attain. For the first time in her life she gets it. With this pain comes a powerful lesson.

Although not perfect, Cindy commits to being mindfully aware of avoiding sarcasm or reserving it for those rare occasions when it will clearly be understood as humour and won't target individuals. She gets the message out of the mess and consciously lets go of this unproductive behaviour.

In your life, look for patterns. Are you being sent messages from the universe or other people again and again and missing them?

Do you keep getting the same discouraging results? What is a repeated disappointment in your life? What irritating factor in your relationships at work or at home keeps raising its head?

Once you recognize the pattern, you're in a position to change it by modifying your own behaviour. When the same or similar situations happen, you'll already know the lesson.

Let go of the mess and keep the message.

Let go guide, Q6: What's the cost of hanging on?

Hanging on can hurt. It takes energy and requires a toll be paid. Remember the monkey bars? It takes as much energy, perhaps more, to keep yourself stationary as it does to move forward. And it's not nearly as satisfying.

The energy you're using to hang on to the pain is energy you could be channeling into more productive activities. Instead of enveloping yourself in misery, you could develop new relationships or deepen your existing ones, seek new career opportunities, or invest more effort in your own healthcare. Maintaining emotional pain takes energy and robs you of opportunities where you could be spending your energies instead.

This opportunity cost, when married with the financial, physical, and emotional costs of hanging on to your status quo painful situation, may be too high. Is it really worth it?

Here's an example that touches many people. It involves the difficult choice to quit smoking.

Smoking Sam

Sam is a really social guy. He loves people and enjoys entertaining. Many years ago, his colleagues encouraged him to take up smoking and now, he desperately wants to quit. His wife doesn't smoke at all and is actually allergic to the vapours.

An incredibly difficult addiction to break, Sam struggles with his fight against nicotine. He sees a doctor and smoking cessation specialist. He uses patches to quelch his desire. He gives hypnotism a shot. He's tries everything anyone recommends and finds that the habit of enjoying cigarettes with his friends is anchored so deeply in his memories, it's difficult to budge.

He asks himself, "What's the cost of hanging on? What am I paying to continue this behaviour of smoking?" He concludes that there is a significant financial cost. In fact, he crunches out that the savings would equate to a trip down south for him and his wife. He knows the physical and health risks if he continues, not to mention the wrinkles and aging it causes. And one cost that he is terrified of is his partner leaving him or, worse yet, causing her to become ill.

These costs are too high for Sam and he recognizes them as motivators to change his actions. He reconciles the risk of losing friends and social times associated with smoking with the fact that his new smoke-free activities aren't against *them, they're* for *him.*

What costs are you paying for the behaviours or beliefs you are holding on to in your life? Maybe it's anger, jealousy, or a sense of injustice that's eating you up. Are you losing sleep and jeopardizing your health because you can't seem to move on? Are these symptoms spilling over into your relationships? It rolls downhill, right? If you feel lousy you release that energy somehow, usually on some unsuspecting and undeserving person in your life you know will take it. You may be ashamed of that behaviour and have lots of reasons to change it.

Perhaps someone is wronging you horribly and unjustly--they are unfaithful, overlook you for promotions and plum projects, or badmouth you constantly. What that person does isn't right at all, maybe unethical, or perhaps even illegal.

Letting it go is a gift to you, not them. It doesn't mean you agree with or condone someone else's behaviour. It means that you acknowledge the resources it takes to hang on and that you'd rather spend those resources moving forward. If the cost is too high, if you are giving up too much to maintain status quo, if your energies are being spent pulling you away from your most coveted goals, let go.

Chapter 8 recap

In this chapter we discussed the price of hanging on and the rewards of letting go. In addition, you now have six salient questions to help you release the pain you may be hanging on to. Not all of them may apply to you and your situation, though I'm pretty sure you that some will ring true and give you new insights. Let's review the highlights and take-aways:

- Hanging on to the past and pain keeps you tethered to the ground;
- It takes as much energy to hang on to the past and pain as it does to move into the future;
- Forgiveness and letting go are gifts you give yourself;
- Use the six questions of the Let Go Guide™ to help you determine if you've earned the right to let it go;
- Letting go isn't *against* them, it's *for* you.

Letting go is no easy task and I congratulate you on considering this option. I sincerely hope that you put the techniques and questions we've discussed here to use. Give yourself permission to let go and fly high. Coming up--a few final thoughts.

CHAPTER 9

FINAL THOUGHTS
Beyond the Finkelstein Factor™

You did it, congratulations! You worked your way through each chapter and exercise and you have arrived at the other end. You now know all about the *Finkelstein Factor*™, how things can go horribly and unfairly wrong, and with the *Flip It Formula*™, you also know what to do about it.

Although this book is ending, your experience and learning continue. As you move forward, life will give you opportunities where you can apply and hone your new coping skills. If you hit a hiccup, just grab this book and refresh your memory on whatever skills or exercise is relevant and will help. No need to remember everything you've covered--it's waiting for you within these pages anytime you want.

What resonates with you, you were meant to hear

Whatever the experience you're living, the messages you are meant and ready to hear have jumped out and will stay with you. When you picked up this book and began reading, you were a different person than who you are now. Maybe you think a little differently or assume an alternate perspective than you did before you were introduced to the stories and strategies I've shared.

FINAL THOUGHTS

Flip It Formula™

STEP 1: Acknowledge the loss

STEP 2: Ask four flippin' questions

- 1) What is **my role**?
- 2) How could it be **worse**?
- 3) What's the **gift**?
- 4) What will I **change in future**?

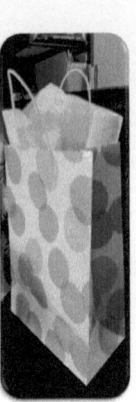

If someone asks you what you got out of this book, what did you learn, what will you say? Whatever pops to mind are your takeaways. Use the *Finkelstein Factor*™ and the *Flip It Formula*™ and these tools will give you confidence and strategies as you face your next challenge.

Sadly, no book, person, or method will have all the answers. That would be too easy, right? You are unique. Your background, personality, education, upbringing, culture, and experiences culminate to create the one and only *you*. As such, certain messages will ring loudly for you and others won't appear as relevant at this time. As your circumstances and you change and evolve, some of the points you didn't think were applicable when you read this book may now be.

One small change can make a big difference

Even if just one strategy speaks to you, that alone will make a difference in your life and how you manage difficult situations. When you make a slight deviation in your direction, the difference may not seem large at the beginning. However, with time, that change is amplified and becomes more distinct. Take a few degrees of difference in a trajectory. That shift can be represented by a pie wedge with one side of the pie being where you originally would have ended up and the other being the new destination with the degrees of change. At the beginning from the starting point, the paths don't look that far apart but when you extend the trajectories, the difference is amplified and you can begin to see that it radically changes the endpoint.

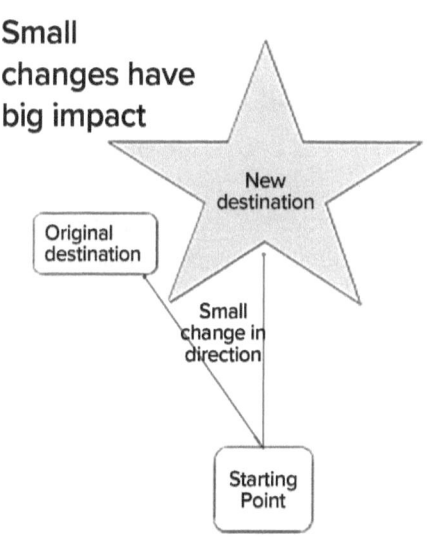

Small changes have big impact

The same is true with the small changes you apply today. They might not seem like much though, with time, they will change dramatically where you end up, physically, emotionally, and potentially in many other ways.

When you change what you think, say, or do-- even in a small way--you change your outcome.

Move knowledge to action

Give it time. Consider what you've read, and when the time is right, apply the tactics and strategies. Only after you've given them due consideration and a chance, then decide if they work for you or not.

Sometimes, it's just that one thing, that single piece of information or way of looking at a situation that will impact your world. Knowledge is only powerful when you move it to action. Pick something, anything from what we've discussed, and apply it to your

FINAL THOUGHTS

life. Take what works for you and forget about the rest ... for now.

Certain phrases, exercises, stories I have shared may stay with you and echo in your mind. You may find yourself applying what you've learned immediately to real-life situations or it may take some time until a circumstance arises that spurs you on to apply your lessons. Grab it. Use it to put into practice and test what you've learned. Find out what works for you and modify what doesn't.

Read again, learn again

This is the type of book you can pick up and put down many times. Even though you're now completing the last chapter, let it not be the last time you visit it. Revisit the sections you want to apply. Remember a particular phrase or exercise that made you think or shift your perception?

You may read this book again from a different perspective and get new meanings. Do it--read it again. Every time you do, you'll pick up something you missed--little beams of light; gems that will guide your way to happier outcomes.

Feedback welcome

Share your takeaway points and let me know what you put into practice and the results you get. What steps, questions, exercises, or thoughts did you find most useful? What suggestions could you offer that would make the *Finkelstein Factor*™ and *Flip It Formula*™ even more powerful and effective? What success stories and impact of implementing these techniques will you share with me? I really want to know how these techniques are received and used and how they impact your life.

Feel free to drop me an email at Marion@MarionSpeaks.com or

visit my website www.MarionSpeaks.com Or if you're planning a conference or workshop and would like me to present on this or other topics, let's chat to explore options.

Before we leave

When I began writing the *Finkelstein Factor*™, I wanted to gather my most useful tips and techniques into one concise communication vehicle to help others. The processes and roadmaps I have shared with you have been developed over the years, applied by hundreds, perhaps thousands of people just like you. They will help you too.

As we draw to a close, for now, I wish you the best in facing and embracing challenging situations with an empowered and enlightened perspective. Not only do you know what to do when things go wrong (because you know they will), you also know you can handle it.

You've got this.

ABOUT THE AUTHOR

Marion Grobb Finkelstein proudly notes that she's been married for three decades—all to the same man, lucky Stephen Finkelstein, the inspiration for the *Finkelstein Factor*™. They live in Niagara Falls, Ontario.

This book, *The Finkelstein Factor*™: *What to do when things go wrong ... because you know they will (sigh)*, marks Marion's first as the sole author, although she's contributed to two anthologies and written many magazines articles and blogs.

As a communication consultant and former Director Communications for national museums, international airports, and Canadian federal institutions, Marion has been dishing out practical, hands-on communication tips and strategies across Canada for decades.

If she's not presenting workplace communication keynotes and workshops at association conferences and corporate client in-house training sessions, Marion is spending summers golfing near her Niagara Falls home or escaping Canadian winters in Florida. She values authentic communication and helps leaders at all levels build teams and leverage their own unique personalities and communication styles.

Marion holds an Honours Bachelor of Administration degree, Marketing Research and Media Communications college certificates, and is also True Colors™ and Personality Dimensions™

ABOUT THE AUTHOR

certified. A long-time member of the Canadian Association of Professional Speakers (CAPS) and Global Speakers Federation (GSF), she is also an award-winning Toastmaster and cablevision producer and recipient of the prestigious Award for Leadership in Service Innovation from the Association of Public Executive Association of Professional Executives of the Public Service of Canada.

Interested in having Marion present at your next conference or employee gathering? Contact her at Marion@MarionSpeaks.com or visit www.MarionSpeaks.com to explore options and opt-in to receive hands-on communication tips enews/blog.

NOTES

www.ingramcontent.com/pod-product-compliance
Lightning Source LLC
Chambersburg PA
CBHW030909080526
44589CB00010B/217